Welcome

One of three Systems Commands within the Department of the Navy, the US Naval Air Systems Command (NAVAIR) has been the principal provider for the Naval Aviation Enterprise (NAE) for six decades. Celebrating its 60th anniversary in 2026, the command's history can be traced back more than 100 years, to the earliest days of US naval aviation.

Established as the successor to the US Navy's Bureau of Naval Weapons, NAVAIR conducts operations across the continental United States. It provides full life-cycle support of naval aviation aircraft, weapons and systems operated by US Naval and US Marine Corps aviation forces. In that role, NAVAIR conducts research, design, development and systems engineering, acquisition, test and evaluation, training facilities/equipment, repair and modification and in-service engineering and logistics support. The command's critical role ensures that the US Navy and Marine Corps have the necessary equipment, training and logistical support to maintain air superiority and achieve their missions. The command's mission is carried out from eight primary locations in the United States and one in Japan, but its workforce can also be found at navy and marine corps air stations.

This special publication examines the organisations, programmes and aircraft that make up the Naval Air Systems Command and support US naval aviation, America's other military organisations and international operators.

Tom Kaminski
Editor

CONTENTS

28

ISBN: 978 1 83632 192 7
Editor: Tom Kaminski
Senior editor, specials: Roger Mortimer
Email: roger.mortimer@keypublishing.com
Cover Design: Steve Donovan
Design: SJmagic DESIGN SERVICES, India
Advertising Sales Manager: Sam Clark
Email: sam.clark@keypublishing.com
Tel: 01780 755131
Advertising Production: Becky Antoniades
Email: Rebecca.antoniades@keypublishing.com

SUBSCRIPTION/MAIL ORDER
Key Publishing Ltd, PO Box 300, Stamford,
Lincs, PE9 1NA
Tel: 01780 480404
Subscriptions email: subs@keypublishing.com
Mail Order email: orders@keypublishing.com
Website: www.keypublishing.com/shop

PUBLISHING
Group CEO: Adrian Cox
Publisher: Steve O'Hara

Published by
Key Publishing Ltd, PO Box 100, Stamford,
Lincs, PE9 1XQ
Tel: 01780 755131
Website: www.keypublishing.com

PRINTING
Precision Colour Printing Ltd, Haldane,
Halesfield 1, Telford, Shropshire.
TF7 4QQ

DISTRIBUTION
Seymour Distribution Ltd, 2 Poultry Avenue,
London, EC1A 9PU
Enquiries Line: 02074 294000.

68

One of three AH-1Z prototypes produced to support the H-1 Upgrades programme undergoes testing at NAS Patuxent River, Maryland, on July 6, 2004. (Tom Kaminski)

Delivering Integrated Air Warfare Capabilities

US Naval Air Systems Command

Headquartered at Naval Air Station (NAS) Patuxent River in Lexington Park, Maryland, since October 1997, the Naval Air Systems Command (NAVAIR) was originally established as the successor to the US Navy's Bureau of Naval Weapons (BUWEPS), which was disestablished on May 1, 1966. It was one of six systems commands aligned under the newly established Naval Material Command (NAVMAC). NAVAIR assumed control over the Naval Air Test Center at NAS Patuxent River, the Naval Missile Center at NAS Point Mugu in California and the Naval Air Engineering Center at NAS Lakehurst, New Jersey. The relationship with NAVMAC ended when the command was disestablished, and NAVAIR was placed directly under the control of the Chief of Naval Operations (CNO) in May 1985. The command has links to the Commandant of the Marine Corps and the Assistant Secretary of the Navy (ASN), Financial Management and Controller (FM&C) and Research Development and Acquisition (RD&A).

NAVAIR's history can be traced to 1921, when the Navy established the Bureau of Aeronautics (BUAER), which was assigned responsibility for the design, procurement and support of naval aircraft. Although the Bureau of Ordnance (BUORD) retained the responsibility for developing airborne weapons, in August 1959 the

two organisations were merged and the BUWEPS was created.

Today the command is responsible for military, civilian and contractor personnel stationed at eight locations across the continental United States and one site overseas. NAVAIR's relocation from Arlington, Virginia, followed the recommendations of the 1993 Base Realignment and Closure (BRAC) Commission. Ground was broken for the first of numerous new facilities at 'Pax River' on February 17, 1995.

NAVAIR delivers "integrated air warfare capabilities to enable the fleet to compete, deter and win – tonight, tomorrow and in the future". This includes full 'cradle to grave' life-cycle support of naval aviation aircraft, weapons and related systems operated by the US Navy and the Marine Corps. Efforts comprise research, design, development and systems engineering, acquisition, test and evaluation, training facilities and equipment, repair and modification and in-service engineering and logistics support. The command has a three-fold role in support of US Naval Aviation:

(Naval Air Systems Command Insignia)

- To develop, acquire and support aircraft, weapons and related systems that can be operated and sustained at sea

- Provide analysis and decision support for cost / schedule / performance trades and investment decisions
- Increase Navy and Marine Corps capability, readiness and affordability in a joint / coalition environment

The command is organised around eight competencies:

- Programme Management
- Contracts
- Research and Engineering
- Test and Evaluation
- Logistics and Industrial Operations
- Corporate Operations
- Comptroller
- Counsel

Vice-Admiral John 'Doc' Dougherty IV assumed command of NAVAIR on August 1, 2025. He previously served as commander of the Naval Air Warfare Center Aircraft Division (NAWCAD) and as NAVAIR's

F-35B test aircraft BF-01 and BF-05 on the forward deck of the amphibious assault ship USS 'Wasp' (LHD 4) during the DT-II phase of development testing on August 12, 2013. (US Navy/Andy Wolfe)

chief engineer. A 1995 graduate of the US Naval Academy, he holds both a Master of Business Administration and Master of Systems Engineering from the Naval Postgraduate School. Dougherty accumulated more than 1,200 hours and 300 carrier landings in the F/A-18C during operational tours. He then went on to senior acquisition roles managing critical programmes including precision strike weapons, F-35 Joint Strike Fighter and the US Navy's Next Generation Air Dominance (NGAD) programme.

During Fiscal Year 2024, NAVAIR received funds totalling $60 billion. Its workforce of 44,600 personnel comprised 30,100 civilian employees, 1,600 military and 12,900 contractors. It was responsible for delivering 107 new aircraft, 22,104 missiles/bombs, 174 unmanned air vehicles/unmanned air systems (UAV/UAS) and five UAV ground systems to US Navy and Marine Corps units. Naval depots carried out maintenance or repairs/upgrades on 454 aircraft, 1,704 engines and more than 30,300 components.

Naval Aviation Enterprise

Formed in 2004, the Naval Aviation Enterprise (NAE) is a collaborative partnership of US Navy and Marine Corps organisations that are individually and collectively responsible for managing and providing all aspects of naval aviation readiness. The enterprise's mission

OV-10A BuNo 155446 was among a number of aircraft types assigned to the Naval Air Test Center Strike Aircraft Test Directorate on October 3, 1983. (Tom Kaminski)

Visiting NAS Glenview, Illinois, during December 2012, NF-14A BuNo 161623 was one of five Tomcats modified in support of the F-14D development programmes. Following its retirement, the aircraft joined the collection of the Patuxent River Naval Air Museum. (Tom Kaminski collection)

Naval Aviation Depot Cherry Point modified a number of F-4S Phantoms to QF-4S configuration including BuNo 157261. The target drones were operated by VX-30 at NAS Point Mugu, California, until retired in 2004. (Tom Kaminski)

Corps organisations that are individually and collectively responsible for managing and providing all aspects of naval aviation readiness. Rather than being represented by a traditional organisational chart with its own funding line, the NAE is a partnership and a way of doing business. Focusing on "collective and collaborative data-driven decision-making, the NAE leverages defined processes, hierarchical metrics and integrated teams to manage naval aviation with an enterprise approach to provide the warfighting readiness". The NAE Strategic Plan is the road map to support naval aviation priorities. It is collaboratively developed to focus on the actions necessary to improve delivery of current and future readiness; streamline and inform and "influence decisions that impact total ownership costs".

NAVAIR organisations

The command is responsible for the Naval Air Warfare Center Aircraft Division (NAWCAD) at NAS Patuxent River, Maryland, Joint Base McGuire-Dix-Lakehurst, New Jersey and Naval Support Activity Orlando, Florida; the Naval Air Warfare Center Weapons Division (NAWCWD) at Naval Base Venture County – Point Mugu and Naval Air Weapons Station (NAWS) China Lake in California; and the Commander, Fleet Readiness Centers (COMFRC) at NAS Patuxent River. The Naval Air Warfare Center Training Systems

is to sustain required current readiness and advance future warfighting capabilities at best possible cost. The Commander Naval Air Forces (CNAF) and the Deputy Commandant for Aviation (DCA) the US Navy and Marine Corps are equal partners in the NAE, and the Commander Naval Air Systems Command (NAVAIR) is the lead provider to the enterprise. In addition to the NAE, NAVAIR contributes to every warfare enterprise in the interest of national security. Formed in 2004, the NAE is a collaborative partnership of Navy and Marine

An EA-18G undergoes testing in the NAWCAD's anechoic chamber. BuNo 169218 was the 151st Growler produced by Boeing. *(US Navy)*

Division (NAWCTSD) in Orlando, Florida, is a subordinate command aligned under the NAWCAD. It provides training systems development for a wide spectrum of military programmes, including aircraft, surface ships, submarines and other specialised requirements.

NAS Pax River hosts more than 50 tenants including three services, federal agencies and private industry. The NAWCAD is the base's largest tenant. It is the US Navy's principal research, development, test and evaluation (RDT&E), engineering and fleet support activity for naval aircraft, engines, avionics, support systems, weapons, fifth-generation weapon system integration and ship/shore/air integration. It delivers a full range of acquisition support for air combat systems ranging from basic research to in-service engineering and logistics. Rear Admiral Todd M Evans has served as the commander of NAWCAD since June 2025. He is also tasked as NAVAIRSYSCOM chief engineer.

NAWCAD's Naval Test Wing Atlantic (NTWL) is composed of four air test and evaluation squadrons and the US Naval Test Pilot School. Together the wing's 4,200 sailors, marines and civilians and organisations support around 140 aircraft from 40 type/model/series (TMS). Three test divisions include air vehicle, mission systems and test management. The Atlantic Test Ranges are fully-instrumented and integrated test ranges that provide full-service support for 'cradle to grave' testing and training. This support includes RDT&E of aircraft, and training for aircrew and integrated avionics and mission systems. Captain Daniel Kitts assumed command as NTWL Commodore on July 2, 2025.

Responsibility for maintaining the facilities at NAS Patuxent River falls under the control of the Navy Region Naval District Washington. The station's air operations department comprises four divisions that support 165,000 air operations annually and manages Pax River's Trapnell Field and the Webster Outlying Field. The divisions comprise air traffic control (ATC), search and rescue (SAR), flight support, airfield management, airfield services division and ground electronic maintenance (GEM). The SAR division is responsible for three Sikorsky MH-60S Seahawks that conduct operations in support of both the air station and local civil SAR call-outs.

The NAWCWD operates from two bases in California: Naval Base Ventura County-Point Mugu and Naval Air Weapons Station (NAWS) China Lake. Headquartered at China Lake, the NAWCWD is responsible for the Naval Test Wing Pacific (NTWP) which has its headquarters at Point Mugu. Individual air test and evaluation squadrons are assigned to each of the facilities. NTWP is responsible for all naval aviation developmental aircraft testing and flight test support on the West Coast. It has responsibility for more than 40 aircraft and is supported by around 670 officer, enlisted, civilian and contractor personnel. Rear Admiral Keith A Hash, who assumed command ▶

An X-47B unmanned combat air system (UCAS) makes an arrested landing aboard the aircraft carrier USS 'George H W Bush' (CVN 77) off the coast of Virginia on July 10, 2013. The landing marked the first time an unmanned autonomous aircraft landed on an aircraft carrier. *(US Navy/Capt Jane E Campbell)*

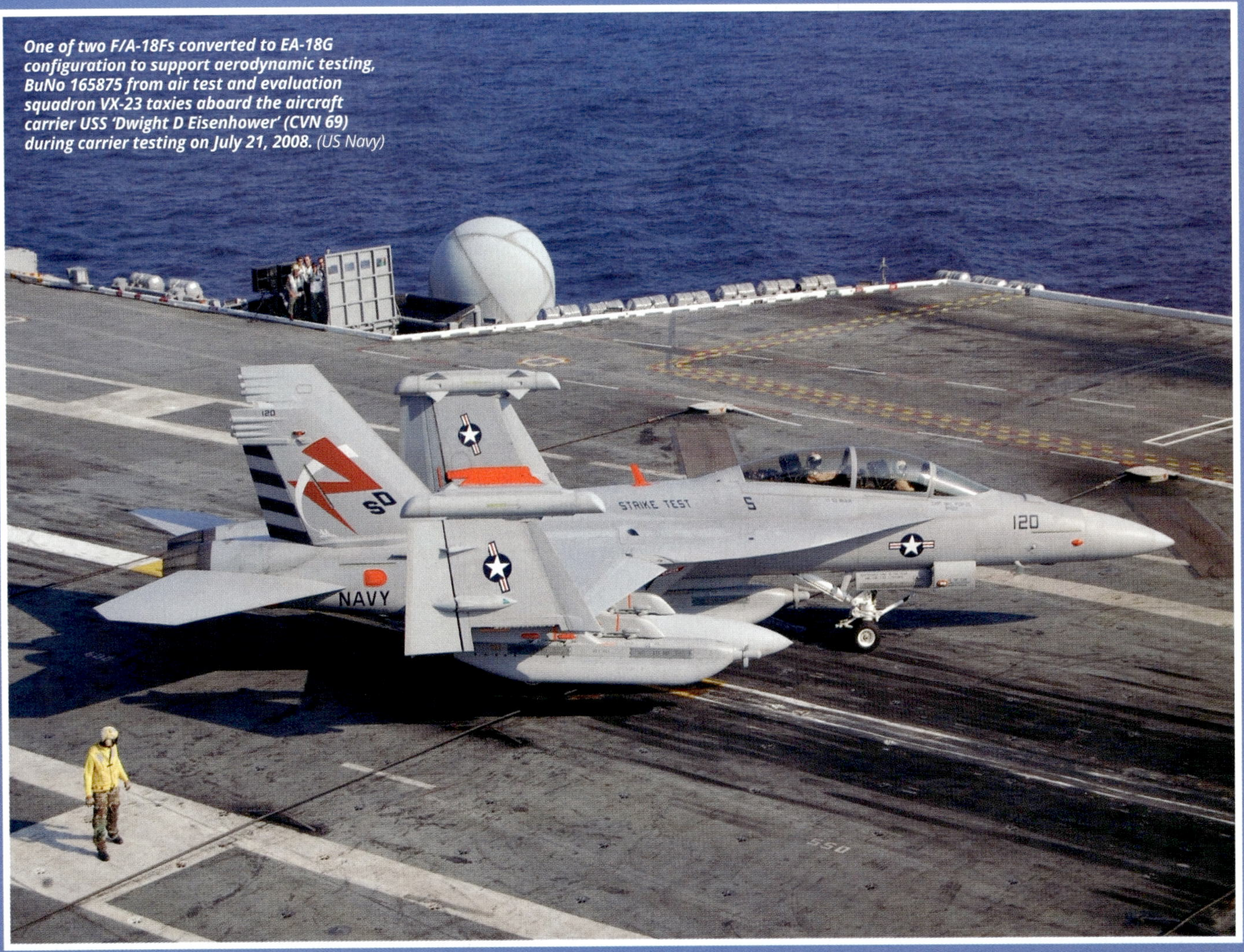

One of two F/A-18Fs converted to EA-18G configuration to support aerodynamic testing, BuNo 165875 from air test and evaluation squadron VX-23 taxies aboard the aircraft carrier USS 'Dwight D Eisenhower' (CVN 69) during carrier testing on July 21, 2008. *(US Navy)*

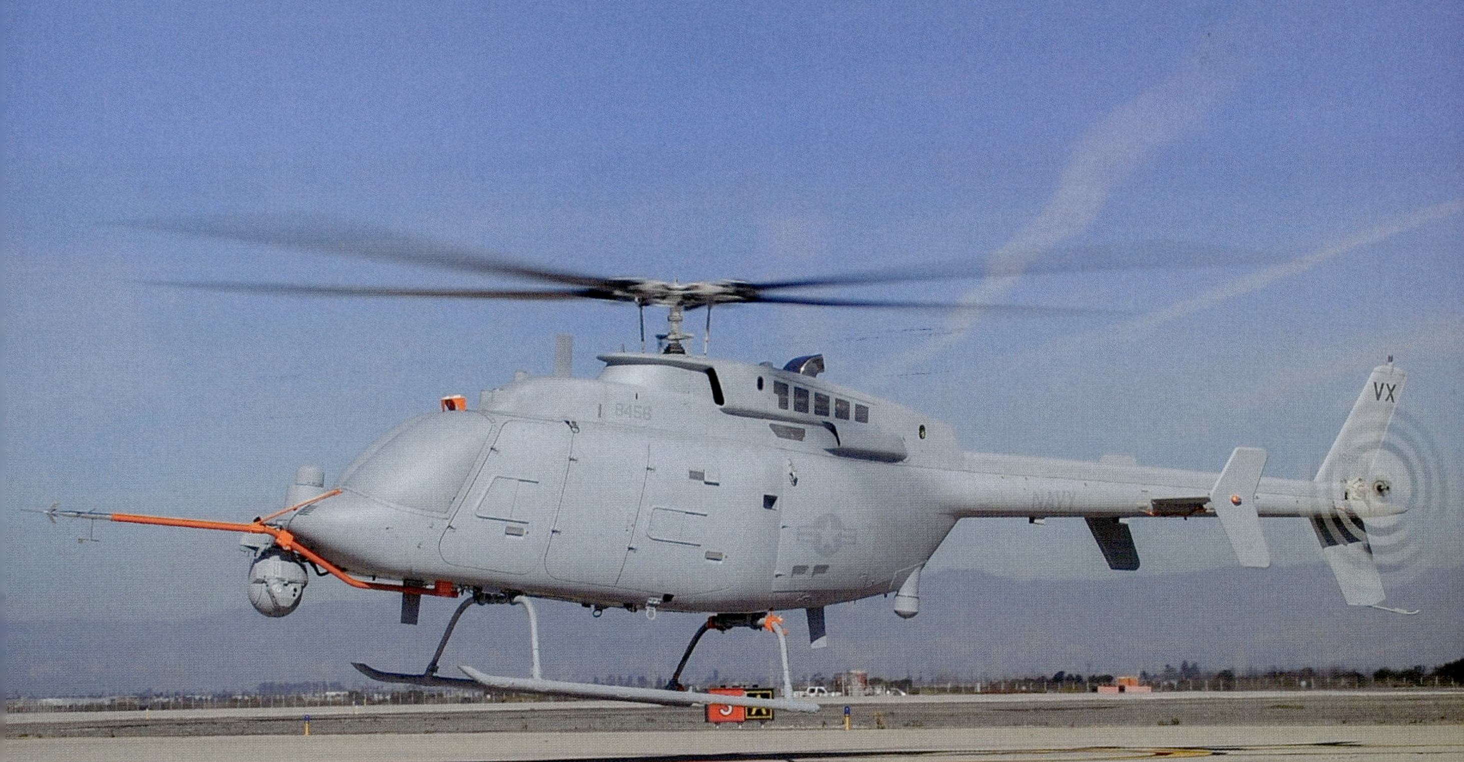

Produced by Northrop Grumman, the MQ-8C was a vertical take-off and landing unmanned aerial vehicle that underwent much of its testing at Naval Base Ventura County Point Mugu, California. Based on the Bell 407 light helicopter, the MQ-8C BuNo 168456 was undergoing testing on February 12, 2014. *(US Navy)*

Commander, Naval Air Systems Command (COMNAVAIRSYSCOM) – NAS Patuxent River, Maryland			
Wing/Squadron	**Location**	**Aircraft**	**Tail Code**
AOD *SAR Dogs* (Note 1)	NAS Patuxent River, Maryland	MH-60S	7A
Naval Air Warfare Center Aircraft Division (NAWCAD) – NAS Patuxent River, Maryland			
Commander, Naval Test Wing Atlantic – NAS Patuxent River, Maryland			
VX-20 *Force*	NAS Patuxent River, Maryland	C-130T, KC-130T/J, E-2C/D, E-6B, T-6A, UC-12M, C-38A, MQ-4C, P-8A,	(WB)
HX-21 *Blackjack*	NAS Patuxent River, Maryland	UH-1Y, AH-1Z, TH-57C, MV-22B, MH-60R/S, CH-53E/K, CMV-22B, VH-92A	HX
VX-23 *Strike*	NAS Patuxent River, Maryland	F/A-18B/C/D/E/F, NF/A-18C/D, T-45C, NEA/EA-18G, F-35B/C	SD
UX-24 *Ghost Wolves*	NOLF Webster Field, St Inigoes, Maryland	RQ-21A, RQ-23A, RQ-26A, MQ-9A	GW
USNTPS	NAS Patuxent River, Maryland	C-12C, F/A-18F, T-6B, AT-6E, T-38C, NU-1B, U-6A, OH-58C, UH-60L, X-26A, UH-72A, C-26A	
Naval Air Warfare Center Weapon Division (NAWCWD) – NAWS China Lake, California			
Commander, Naval Test Wing Pacific – NB Ventura County Point Mugu, California			
VX-30 *Bloodhounds*	NB Ventura County Point Mugu, California	NP/P-3C, KC-130T, NRQ-21A, RQ-23A, NC-20G, E-2D	BH
VX-31 *Dust Devils*	NAWS China Lake, California	F/A-18C/D/E/F, NEA/EA-18G, AV-8B+, MH-60S, MQ-9A	DD
Commander, Fleet Readiness Centers (COMFRC) – NAS Patuxent River, Maryland			
FRC East	MCAS Cherry Point, North Carolina	(No aircraft assigned)	
FRC Mid-Atlantic	NAS Oceana, Virginia	(No aircraft assigned)	
FRC Southeast	NAS Jacksonville, Florida	(No aircraft assigned)	
FRC Northwest	NAS Whidbey Island, Washington	(No aircraft assigned)	
FRC Southwest	NAS North Island, California	(No aircraft assigned)	
FRC West	NAS Lemoore, California	(No aircraft assigned)	
FRC Western Pacific	NAF Atsugi, Japan	(No aircraft assigned)	
FRC Reserve Mid-West	NAS JRB Fort Worth, Texas	(No aircraft assigned)	

Note

1 The NAS Patuxent River Air Operations Department is responsible for the Search and Rescue Division's MH-60S helicopters.

Abbreviations

AOD	Air Operations Department	NAWC	Naval Air Warfare Center
FRC	Fleet Readiness Center	NAWS	Naval Air Weapons Station
HX	Air Test & Evaluation Squadron	NB	Naval Base
JRB	Joint Reserve Base	NOLF	Naval Outlying Field
MCAS	Marine Corps Air Station	USNTPS	US Naval Test Pilot School
NAF	Naval Air Facility	UX	Air Test & Evaluation Squadron (Unmanned)
NAS	Naval Air Station	VX	Air Test & Evaluation Squadron

Aircraft sold under foreign military sales programmes often undergo testing prior to delivery. Recently, the Indian Navy's MH-60R was at Patuxent River for testing in the anechoic chamber. (US Navy)

MV-22B BuNo 165443 undergoes testing with the Osprey Integrated Test Team at NAS Patuxent River in October 2022. The aircraft is now located at NAS North Island, California, where it serves as a loads trainer. (Tom Kaminski)

Program Executive Officers

Through an operating agreement with the assistant secretary of the navy (RD&A), NAVAIR provides support, comprising personnel, processes, tools, training, mission facilities and core technologies to naval aviation Program Executive Officers (PEOs).

PEOs are responsible for the full lifecycle of naval aircraft and weapons programmes, from research and development to procurement, fielding and sustainment. Along with their assigned programme managers, the PEOs are responsible for achieving the cost, schedule and performance requirements for their assigned programmes. Each PEO oversees the work carried out by numerous programme offices that are designated as a numbered Program Manager Air (PMA):

- PEO Tactical Aircraft Programs (PEO-T) - Aircraft, weapons and systems
  - PMA-205: Naval Aviation Training Systems and Ranges
  - PMA-209: Air Combat Electronics
  - PMA-213: Naval Air Traffic Management Systems
  - PMA-226: Specialised and Proven Aircraft
  - PMA-213: Naval Air Traffic Management Systems
  - PMA-230: Next Generation Air Dominance
  - PMA-231: E-2/C-2 Airborne Command and Control Systems
  - PMA-234: Airborne Electronic Attack Systems
  - PMA-251: Aircraft Launch and Recovery Equipment
  - PMA-257: AV-8B
  - PMA-265: F/A-18 and EA-18G
  - PMA-272: Advanced Tactical Aircraft Protection Systems
  - PMA-273: Naval Undergraduate Flight Training Systems

of NAWCWD in June 2022, is also NAVAIR assistant commander for test and evaluation. Since July 2023, responsibility for NTWP has been assigned to Captain David M Halpern. As NTWP commodore, he is responsible for two air test and evaluation squadrons.

The facilities at both Naval Base Ventura County Point Mugu and NAWS China Lake fall under the control of the commander of Navy Region Southwest, which is part of the US Pacific Fleet. The airfields at both locations are operated by their respective air operations departments, which provide air traffic control (ATC), air terminal, field facilities and ground electronic maintenance services to support the base's tenants and visitors. The ATC facility at Point Mugu is the most complex operation of its type in the US Navy. It has jurisdiction of more than 3,000 miles of airspace from the surface to 8,000ft and works closely with the sea test range and the Federal Aviation Administration. More than 20,000 manned and unmanned military sorties are conducted from China Lake's Armitage Field by US Armed Forces each year and Point Mugu controls more than 150,000 military and civilian flight operations annually.

An F-35C test aircraft CF-03 approaches the aircraft carrier USS 'Nimitz' (CVN 68) for an arrested landing on November 3, 2014. The Lightning II was one of two that was supporting testing aboard 'Nimitz'. (US Navy/Andy Wolfe)

The third developmental F/A-18A was assigned to the Naval Air Test Center's Strike Aircraft Test Directorate while undergoing testing at NAS Patuxent River on October 3, 1983. *(Tom Kaminski)*

- PEO Air Anti-Submarine Warfare, Assault and Special Mission Programs – PEO(A) – helicopters, tactical airlift, special mission aircraft and aviation anti-submarine warfare equipment and aircraft
  - PMA-207: Tactical Airlift
  - PMA-261: H-53 Heavy Lift Helicopters
  - PMA-264: Air Anti-Submarine Warfare Systems
  - PMA-271: Airborne Strategic Command, Control and Communications
  - PMA-274: Presidential Helicopters
  - PMA-275: V-22 Joint Program Office
  - PMA-276: Light/Attack Helicopters
  - PMA-290: Maritime Patrol and Reconnaissance Aircraft (MPRA)
  - PMA-299: H-60 Multi-mission Helicopters
- PEO Unmanned Aviation and Strike Weapons – PEO(U&W) – Unmanned aircraft, weapons and target systems
  - PMA-201: Precision Strike Weapons
  - PMA-202: Aircrew Systems
  - PMA-208: Aerial Targets
  - PMA-242: Direct and Time Sensitive Strike
  - PMA-259: Air-To-Air Missiles
  - PMA-260: Common Aviation Support Equipment
  - PMA-262: Persistent Maritime Unmanned Aircraft Systems
  - PMA-263: Navy and Marine Corps Small Tactical Unmanned Aircraft Systems
  - PMA-266: Multi-Mission Tactical Unmanned Aerial Systems (UAS)
  - PMA-268: Unmanned Carrier Aviation
  - PMA-280: Tomahawk Weapons System
  - PMA-281: Strike Planning and Execution Systems
- PEO Joint Strike Fighter
  - PEO(JSF) – Also known as the Joint Strike Fighter Program, the F-35 Lightning II Joint Program Office (JPO) leads the life-cycle programme management of the F-35A, F-35B and the F-35C for the US Air Force, US Marine Corps, US Navy, international partners and foreign military sales customers

International programmes

The Security Co-operation Office (SSCO) works with 30 programme offices and six field sites, managing a portfolio of 1,243 open cases for 71 countries, with an overall value of $96bn. It generated sales of $13.5bn during Fiscal Year 2024. ∎

An EA-6B from the 'Salty Dogs' of Air Test and Evaluation Squadron VX-23 flies over southern Maryland on a biofuel blend of JP-5 aviation fuel and camelina oil. VX-23 retired its last Prowler in August 2017 and BuNo 159909 is now part of the collection of the Patuxent River Naval Air Museum. *(US Navy/Kelly Schindler)*

Former EC-130G BuNo 151891 served the US Naval Air Test Center's Antisubmarine Aircraft Test Directorate after being replaced by the EC-130Q version operationally. *(Tom Kaminski)*

A TA-7C flown by the flight test division of the Pacific Missile Test Center on the ramp at NAS Point Mugu, California, on October 11, 1990. LTV converted 24 A-7Bs and 36 A-7Cs Corsair IIs to the two-seat trainer configuration. Initially operated by fleet replacement squadrons, a number of the aircraft went on to serve in test and support roles. *(Mike Anselmo)*

US NAVAL AIR SYSTEMS COMMAND ASSOCIATED FACILITIES

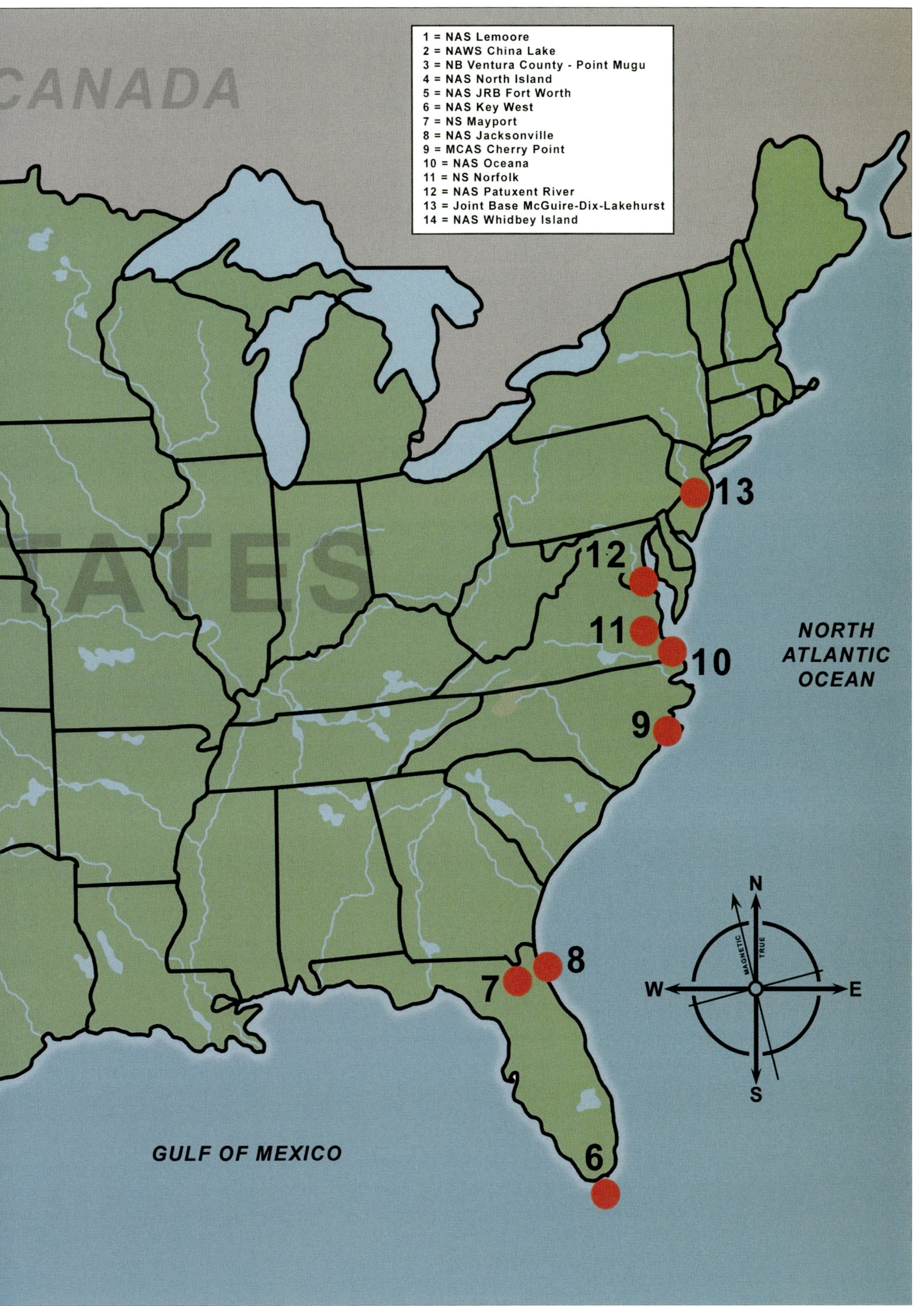

CANADA
1 = NAS Lemoore
2 = NAWS China Lake
3 = NB Ventura County - Point Mugu
4 = NAS North Island
5 = NAS JRB Fort Worth
6 = NAS Key West
7 = NS Mayport
8 = NAS Jacksonville
9 = MCAS Cherry Point
10 = NAS Oceana
11 = NS Norfolk
12 = NAS Patuxent River
13 = Joint Base McGuire-Dix-Lakehurst
14 = NAS Whidbey Island
STATES
NORTH ATLANTIC OCEAN
13
12
11
10
9
8
7
6
N
S
E
W
MAGNETIC
TRUE
GULF OF MEXICO

Where Flight

US Naval Air Warfare Center Aircraft Division (NAWCAD)

Located in Lexington Park, Maryland, Naval Air Station (NAS) Patuxent River, is one of four US Navy aviation facilities supporting the research, development, test and evaluation (RDT&E) and operational, test and evaluation (OT&E) of new and deployed naval aircraft and weapon systems. Shortly after 'Pax River' was commissioned on April 1, 1943, flight, radio and experimental and development squadrons that had been based at NAS Anacostia in the District of Columbia and an aircraft armament test unit from NAS Norfolk, Virginia, relocated to the station. With the moves completed that August, these organisations were assigned to electronics, armament, flight and tactical test divisions and later during 1944 a service test unit was also activated at Pax River. The test activities were formally consolidated under a single organisation when the US Naval Air Test Center (NATC) was established on June 16, 1945.

During 1953, the functions of the tactical and service test divisions were merged under the Service Test Division. Establishment of the US Naval Test Pilot School followed in 1958. The armament and electronics test divisions were similarly consolidated to form the Weapons Systems Test Division in 1960. The first major reorganisation of the NATC took place on April 1, 1975, when its three test divisions were inactivated and replaced by the Strike, Antisubmarine and Rotary Wing Aircraft Test Directorates and the Systems Engineering Test Directorate. A major reorganisation occurred on January 1, 1992, when the Naval Air Development Center (NADC) at Warminster in Pennsylvania, Naval Air Engineering Center (NAEC) at Lakehurst in New Jersey, Naval Air Propulsion Center (NAPC) at Trenton in New Jersey, the Naval Avionics Center (NAC) at Indianapolis, Indiana and the NATC

were all disestablished. Their assets were combined under the newly created Naval Air Warfare Center Aircraft Division (NAWCAD), headquartered at Patuxent River.

Naval Test Wing Atlantic

When the new organisation was formed, NATC's test directorates were arranged as part of the NAWCAD's Flight Test Engineering Group (FTEG). However, on July 31, 1995, Commander

Naval Test Wing Atlantic (NTWL) was formally established under NAWCAD and assumed control of the NATC's Naval Force, Naval Rotary Wing and Naval Strike Aircraft Test Squadrons just days earlier. The wing also assumed responsibility for the Naval Test Pilot School, the Atlantic Ranges and Facilities and an Aircraft Intermediate Maintenance Department (AIMD). The most recent reorganisation was on May 1, 2002, when the three Aircraft Test Squadrons

ABOVE: *The Northrop Grumman X-47B unmanned combat air system demonstrator lands at NAS Patuxent Rive, on May 14, 2013, after completing the first launch of an unmanned aerial vehicle from an aircraft carrier. (US Navy/Kelly Schindler*

BELOW: *E-2D BuNo 166501 is prepared for launch using the land-based electromagnetic aircraft launch system (EMALS) at NAWCAD's full-size shipboard-representative test site at Joint Base McGuire-Dix-Lakehurst, New Jersey, on September 27, 2011. Known as AA-01, the first Advanced Hawkeye is operated by Air Test and Evaluation Squadron VX-20 from NAS Patuxent River, Maryland. (US Navy/Kelly Schindler)*

Test Happens

(Naval Air Warfare Center Aircraft Division Insignia)

were respectively redesignated at Air Test and Evaluation Squadrons VX-20, HX-21 and VX-23. A fourth squadron joined the wing when Air Test & Evaluation Squadron Two Four (UX-24) was established on October 18, 2018, at Patuxent River's Webster Field Annex in St Inigoes, Maryland. Officially known as Navy Outlying Field (NOLF) Webster, the facility is around 15 miles (24km) south of NAS Patuxent River; Webster Field covers around 850 acres between St Inigoes Creek to the northeast and St Mary's River on the north and west.

NTWL is the most technically diverse air wing in naval aviation and manages test and evaluation of aviation systems ranging from unmanned to rotary and fixed-wing aircraft and subsystems. The wing is also responsible for the US Naval Test Pilot School at Pax River.

NAWC-AD conducts RDT&E and sustainment flight testing for all US Navy and Marine Corps aircraft and aircraft systems. In addition to the test wing, it is responsible for ranges, facilities, laboratories and aircraft that support its mission. As well as the facilities and organisations at Pax River, NAWCAD also maintains facilities at St Inigoes and Lakehurst. Additionally, its propulsion and power facilities conduct testing of propulsion systems and other components for naval aircraft systems and those of other services and research agencies.

NAWCAD has extensive airfields, flight test ranges, aircraft systems test facilities and simulation laboratories to support aircraft RDT&E. This includes nearly 60,000sq miles (155,399km²) of airspace, 39,375sq miles (101,981km²) of sea space and 7,950 acres of land space. Product areas include aircraft systems flight test and evaluation, carrier suitability certification, test article preparation, installed system test and evaluation and modelling and simulation support of the acquisition process. The Test and Evaluation Group at Pax River performs DT&E and OT&E of manned and unmanned air vehicle systems, including mission systems, equipment, subsystems, components and support systems. This project also provides test and evaluation facilities for air-breathing propulsion systems and extensive facilities for conducting both

installed and uninstalled aircraft engine development and test and evaluation.

The wing and its subordinate test squadrons are responsible for conducting DT&E and engineering for newly developed aircraft, engines, avionics and aircraft support equipment destined for service with the US Navy and Marine Corps and test and evaluation (T&E) in support of mature programmes. The wing is responsible for conducting a variety of flight and ground tests that confirm an aircraft or weapon system's airworthiness and ability to carry out its missions. NAWCAD also supports contractor tests and those associated with foreign aircraft.

Aircraft operated by the three test squadrons include representative fleet aircraft and those that have been permanently modified for flight test duties and many are equipped with instrumentation and telemetry systems. Examples of the tests include carrier and shipboard suitability, propulsion and aircraft mission systems testing, ordnance compatibility and ballistics efforts, reliability and maintainability assessments, flight simulation and flight control software development. While DT&E serves as a demonstration that an aircraft, or its related system, meets design specifications and ensures it is ready for operational testing (OT) by fleet operators, the successful completion of OT results in full rate production and fleet introduction. In addition, the squadrons support initial flight testing of new aircraft during the engineering manufacturing development (EMD) and operational evaluations (OPEVAL) phases. ▶

E-2D BuNo 168077 makes an arrested landing using the land-based advanced arresting gear (AAG) at NAWCAD's runway arrested landing site (RALS) test site at Joint Base McGuire-Dix-Lakehurst on September 27, 2011. (US Navy)

Testing

There is a considerable amount of overlap between the EMD, DT&E and T&E flight tests, which may include all or some of the following:

- Performance tests – Confirm an aircraft's take-off, climb, cruise, hover, combat, descent and landing capabilities.
- Flying qualities or handling qualities tests – Determine the aircraft's ability to carry out its mission, verify it meets specification requirements, define its airworthiness and safe operating envelope and stability and controllability characteristics. Besides conducting these tests on fully operational airframes, extensive testing is conducted with one or more of the aircraft's major systems, such as engines, avionics and flight control systems.
- Structural loads tests – Provide a means to measure structural loads and strain data used to verify the structural integrity of the aircraft's primary and secondary structural components and include ground and flight test manoeuvres.
- Stability and control tests – Measure the aircraft's conformance with its specification requirements and include static and dynamic directional tests, manoeuvring stability tests and control power tests.
- Envelope expansion tests – Determine the aircraft's maximum safe and effective operating capabilities. Tests are performed on new aircraft and others that have received modifications that affect flight envelopes including airspeed, mach, acceleration, angle of attack and engine limits.
- High angle of attack tests – Measure and evaluate handling qualities, controllability and manoeuvring capabilities at lower than normal

ABOVE AND BELOW: *An F-35B performs a short take-off launch conducted by the F-35 Integrated Test Force (ITF) from the land-based ski jump at NAS Patuxent River on February 16, 2022. BuNo 168717 was operated by Air Test and Evaluation VX-23.* (US Navy/Kyra Helwick)

The first production F-35A for the Italian Air Force arrived at Pax River on February 5, 2016, marking the first transatlantic crossing for the Lightning II. Built at the Cameri Final Assembly and Check-Out (FACO) facility, serial MM7332 underwent electromagnetic environmental effects testing in NAWCAD's anechoic chamber. (US Navy Andy Wolfe)

The fourth production F/A-18E taxies back to the ramp at Pax River after a flight on April 4, 1997. Super Hornet BuNo 168168 was specially configured to support spin testing. (Tom Kaminski)

airspeeds and/or at higher than normal angles of attack and determine an aircraft's resistance to departure from controlled flight, control recovery and spin characteristics. These are often referred to a 'high alpha' tests.

• Carrier suitability testing – Primarily meant to determine the suitability of fixed-wing carrier-based aircraft and its systems for catapult launch and arrested landing operations. During 'carrier suit', the aircraft is tested at varying speeds up to its published catapult launch and arrested landing limits and subjected to wave-offs, stores certification, taxiing, performance, aircraft steam ingestion testing, aircraft carrier catapult and arresting gear certifications, aircraft approach handling qualities and launch and recovery envelope expansion. Any new aircraft configuration (ie system or weapon) is subjected to a standard battery of arrestments that include high-sink rate landings, free-flight and aircraft roll and yaw at engagement, and maximum longitudinal-g on arrestment. Tests are conducted at glide slopes that range from two to six degrees and at speeds as high as the aircraft and arresting gear's maximum design.

• Rotary-wing ship suitability – Determines the compatibility of helicopters and tiltrotor aircraft with the shipboard operating environment. This includes compatibility with visual and mechanical landing systems such as the recovery assist secure and traverse (RAST) system that equips most destroyers, cruisers and frigates. Dynamic interface (DI) testing evaluates the suitability of a helicopter to operate on and around a ship and includes a combination of simulation, land-based facilities and actual landings on ships at sea. The tests are designed to determine distinctive performance capabilities and limitations associated with unique motion, air wake and fight deck physical parameters associated with each class of ship. The results support the development of shipboard helicopter launch and recovery operations envelopes.

An F-35B's short take-off launch conducted by the ITF at Pax River, February 9, 2021, test aircraft BF-03 operated by VX-23. (US Navy/Kyra Helwick)

- Aircraft stores compatibility tests – Determine the ability of an aircraft, store and related suspension equipment to interface without causing unacceptable effects and are conducted throughout the ground and flight conditions that the combination would be subjected to.
- Captive carriage tests – Evaluate the installation of a store or suspension equipment on an aircraft under all flight and ground conditions including taxi, take-off and landing to determine the integrity of the installation and ensure that the aircraft's stability and control is acceptable.
- Separation tests – Verify that a store is able separate from an aircraft without exceeding the design limits of the store or the aircraft and without contacting or otherwise damaging the aircraft, suspension equipment or other released and unreleased stores.
- Jettison testing – Evaluates the intentional 'safe' release of stores, suspension equipment, expended rocket pods, fuel tanks or hung bombs from the aircraft that are no longer required for the performance of the mission or may pose a threat to safe flight.
- Store launching and weapon release tests – Investigates the intentional separation of self-propelled stores such as a missiles, rockets or target-drones or free-fall stores, such as bombs.

In addition to flight testing the aircraft, its avionics and weapon systems are subjected to

The third of four F-35C Carrier Variant test aircraft flies over NAS Patuxent River during its delivery flight to the Maryland facility on June 2, 2011. Lockheed Martin

TOP TO BOTTOM: *F-35C test aircraft CF-05 'traps' at Naval Air Warfare Center Aircraft Division–Lakehurst's runway arrested landing site (RALS) on February 27, 2024. RALS is a shipboard-representative test site that features a land-based version of the advanced arresting gear that equips the US Navy's Ford-class of aircraft carriers.* (US Navy)

a series of ground tests that confirm they meet design requirements such as detection range, processing speeds and mean time between failures. They also must demonstrate their operation without interfering with one another and without interference from outside sources.

Test facilities and laboratories include the Air Combat Environment Test and Evaluation Facility (ACETEF), which creates virtual battlespace environments to test and evaluate electronic warfare systems. The facility partially comprises the Simulated Warfare Environment Generator (SWEG), Manned Flight Simulator (MFS), Electronic Warfare Integrated Systems Test Laboratory (EWISTL), offensive sensors and communication, navigation and identification (CNI) laboratories, anechoic chamber and a shielded hangar.

Atlantic Ranges and Targets

The Atlantic Ranges and Targets (ART) organisation manages services on land, at sea and in the air across the eastern seaboard, and at defence and industry ranges and test sites worldwide. ART provides the range facilities, maritime platforms, targets and instrumentation that support test and training environments.

It schedules and controls land, sea and air associated range operating areas and provides range resources and threat-representative target presentations for conducting research, development, test, evaluation, experimentation and training in support of naval aviation and warfighters.

ART works with the US Department of Defense (DoD) and industry to provide command and control expertise and data collection and analysis

An F/A-18E is prepared for launching from the electromagnetic aircraft launch system at NAWCAD Lakehurst's facility aboard Joint Base McGuire-Dix-Lakehurst, New Jersey, on June 8, 2017.
(US Navy /Kelly Schindler)

tools for flight test activities and major live, virtual and constructive experimentation events.

The Atlantic Test Range (ATR) is the US Navy's East Coast open-air test range. It provides the airspace, data-gathering equipment and instrumentation for aviation and weapons systems test and evaluation, warfighter training and experimentation events.

Local tests are conducted in 2,700sq miles (6,993km²) of restricted airspace in and around the Chesapeake Bay that range up to an altitude of 85,000ft (2,598m). An additional 57,000sq miles (147,629km²) of air and sea space is also available

offshore over the Atlantic Ocean in an area that extends from New Jersey to the Carolinas, where altitude is unlimited. Real-time connectivity and partnerships with other defence entities allow ATR to extend its range and capabilities.

Atlantic Targets and Marine Operations (ATMO) provides targets and marine services needed to support aircraft and weapons research, development, test, evaluation, experimentation and warfighter training events. Activities in Maryland, Virginia and Florida provide the staff, equipment and facilities that create realistic threat simulations in air, land and ▶

A T-45C began AAG performance testing at the RALS at Joint Base McGuire-Dix-Lakehurst on August 13, 2019. (US Navy)

sea environments. The organisation designs, develops and modifies target systems and deploys a range of vessels that support unique maritime requirements.

The ART is responsible for surveillance and telemetry equipment and the many laboratories and test sites on the air station. These facilities are assigned to divisions within the organisation:

- Range Operations is responsible for airspace management, test communications and marine operations and targets.
- Range Instrumentation operates and maintains systems that track and record time space position information, electronic warfare and radar cross section, telemetry and photogrametrics or photographic measuring data.
- Test and Training Programs is tasked with systems development, fleet support and training range development.
- Propulsion Test and Evaluation operates and maintains test systems for engines and

components and test environment and instrumentation.
- Aircraft Simulation is responsible for avionics simulation and simulator systems that include warfare and electronic combat simulation.
- Electromagnetic Environmental Effects (electromagnetic compatibility, electromagnetic effects)

Support equipment associated with the ranges includes acquisition, surveillance, instrumented tracking and special purpose radar systems; videographic and photographic instrumentation, optical and laser tracking systems; aerial, sea and land targets; and time, space, position information systems. A multiple-object tracking system permits testing of numerous air-surface tests over the two ranges. Additionally, a range computation and control facility integrates telemetry data from test aircraft with digital tracking data to provide the high accuracy, multi-stream, real-time data

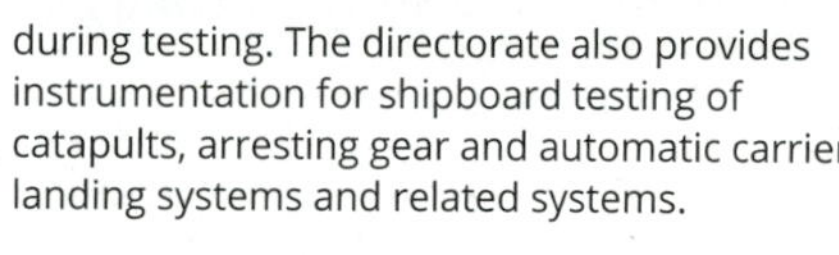

during testing. The directorate also provides instrumentation for shipboard testing of catapults, arresting gear and automatic carrier landing systems and related systems.

Lakehurst

Joint Base McGuire-Dix-Lakehurst (JBMDL), in central New Jersey, is home to NAWCAD Lakehurst, which is the world leader in aircraft launch and recovery equipment (ALRE) and naval aviation support equipment (SE). It conducts acquisition management, technology development, systems integration, engineering, rapid prototyping / manufacturing, developmental evaluation and verification, fleet engineering support and integrated logistics support management. NAWCAD Lakehurst is responsible for both fleet support and developing technology that permits fixed and rotary-wing aircraft to operate safely and effectively from aircraft carriers, air capable ships and expeditionary airfields worldwide.

ALRE includes catapults/launching systems, jet blast deflectors, arresting gear, visual landing aids, information systems and matting, recovery systems, landing aids and airfield lighting associated with expeditionary airfields (EAF). SE is associated with avionics that include advanced diagnostics, aircraft handling, servicing and maintenance, propulsion, maintenance information systems and weapons handling equipment.

The US Navy's AAG programme reached a milestone with the first recovery of a manned aircraft, when an F/A-18E snagged the arresting wire at the runway arrested landing site on March 31, 2016. The facility is located aboard Joint Base McGuire-Dix-Lakehurst in New Jersey but is operated by the NAWCAD. (US Navy)

An F/A18F assigned to Air Test and Evaluation Squadron VX-23 conducts air refuelling tests with a German Air Force A400M Atlas on January 11, 2024. The test was intended to certify the Super Hornet and EA-18G Growler to refuel from the Atlas. BuNo 165801 wore a special paint scheme celebrating VX-23's markings. (US Navy/Erik Hildebrandt)

The Lakehurst site occupies around 7,430 of the 42,000 acres comprising the joint base that includes Lakehurst Maxfield Field's 12,000ft (3,658m) dedicated RDT&E runway. The runway houses two fleet representative TC-13 steam catapults, an aircraft carrier electromagnetic aircraft launch system (EMALS), Mk-7 arresting gear and advanced arresting gear (AAG) systems. A jet blast deflector and shore-based arresting gear are also part of the test complex. Three active mile-and-a-quarter-long jet car test tracks equipped with recovery systems simulate aircraft recovery by propelling dead loads weighing up to 100,000lb (45,359kg) into arresting gear.

EMALS and AAG were first fielded aboard the nuclear-powered aircraft carrier USS *Gerald R Ford* (CVN 78). The first live aircraft launch from Lakehurst's land-based EMALS was on December 18, 2010, when an F/A-18E from VX-23 was catapulted. The first recovery using the AAG followed on May 31, 2016, when another VX-23 Super Hornet was 'trapped'.

EAF equipment includes aircraft recovery systems such as the M31 Marine Corps Expeditionary Arresting Gear System (MCEAGS) and E28 Emergency Runway Arresting Gear.

Located near Lakehurst's test runway, the elevated fixed platform (EFP) is a full-scale elevated landing pad that originally replicated the flight deck of a US Navy FFG 7-class guided missile frigate. Used for dynamic interface (DI) testing, the EFP measures 60 x 85ft (18.29 x 25.9m) and features a simulated shipboard hangar face. In addition to visual landing aids (VLA) lighting and markings it is equipped with a recovery assist, securing and traversing (RAST) system. The site can support helicopters weighing up to 90,000lb (40,823kg) landing at a maximum sink rate of 2.67Gs.

Commissioned in 2020, the ship motion platform (SMP) supports the development and testing of unmanned aerial vehicles/unmanned air systems (UAV/UAS) for launch and recovery from ships at sea. It can simulate the ▶

NAWCAD's land-based EMALS successfully completed the first launch of a T-45C trainer from the NAVAIR Lakehurst test site on June 1, 2011. Twelve successful Goshawk launches were conducted on June 1 and 2 as part of the aircraft compatibility testing. (US Navy)

movement of aircraft carriers and guided-missile destroyers in waves up to sea state four with wave heights of 4ft to 8ft.

Additional facilities at Lakehurst include more than 20 advanced engineering labs, training facilities and advanced manufacturing capability and rapid prototyping shops.

Construction of new facilities that will house a joint precision approach and landing system (JPALS) and an unmanned carrier aviation mission control system for the MQ-25A and other aircraft programmes began at Lakehurst in January 2025.

Famous as the crash site of the German airship *Hindenburg* on May 6, 1937, the former NAS Lakehurst served the US Navy as a 'lighter-than-air' base from 1921 to 1961. Tasked to test and evaluate aircraft launch and recovery systems and aviation support equipment, the Naval Air Test Facility (NATF) was established as a tenant at Lakehurst in 1957. The former Naval Aircraft Factory moved from Philadelphia to Lakehurst in 1973 and was renamed the Naval Air Engineering Center (NAEC). In 1977, NATF and NAS Lakehurst were aligned under the NAEC.

Renamed again as the Naval Air Engineering Station Lakehurst in 1992, the facility was realigned to become part of the tri-service JBMDL on October 1, 2009.

AIRWorks

As NAWCAD's rapid capability office, AIRWorks is focused on quickly delivering fast, cost-effective, quality solutions to meet immediate and emergent warfighter needs. Its services include aircraft modification, prototyping, additive manufacturing (3D printing), systems integration, sustainment, intelligence, surveillance and reconnaissance and rapid contracting.

Delivering engineering, procurement and programme management, AIRWorks helps acquisition offices expedite contracting and accelerate development of new technology, and deliver high-quality solutions at an affordable cost as an organic lead systems integrator. By delivering high-quality affordable solutions, AIRWorks is leading the effort to expedite a shift towards delivering better, faster and more cost-effective solutions for warfighters.

AIRWorks recently led systems integration for the US Marine Corps, which rapidly modified two Kratos XQ-58A experimental unmanned

A pilot trains in the Naval Air Warfare Center Aircraft Division Joint Simulation Environment (JSE) at NAS Patuxent River, Maryland. Tactical pilots from the US Marine Corps and Air Force conducted the first-ever joint training exercise flying simulated combat missions together in F-35 and F-22 fifth-generation fighter jets in the JSE in March 2024. (US Navy/Terri Thomas)

combat aerial vehicles (UCAV) that subsequently completed three test events and a capstone demonstration/joint exercise event validating the Valkyrie's potential combat collaborative aircraft capability as part of the service's Penetrating Affordable Autonomous Collaborative Killer – Portfolio (PAACK-P) programme.

Training systems

Headquartered at Naval Support Activity Orlando, Florida, the Naval Air Warfare Center Training Systems Division (NAWCTSD) is the US Navy's primary source for a wide spectrum of training solutions for the warfighter that includes aviation, undersea, surface warfare and cross warfare systems.

The Program Director for Aviation (PDA) is aligned with NAWCTSD and the NAVAIR Training Systems Program Manager (PMA-205) for management of Naval and Marine Corps aviation training programmes, systems and products related to aviation weapons systems, platforms and environment. Responsibilities include aircraft, armament, air traffic control, aviation systems and other related equipment. PDA provides support for aviation-related training provided by the Naval Education and

Training Command (NETC) and its subordinate commands. NAWCTSD traces its roots to the 1941 creation of the Special Devices Desk in the US Navy Bureau of Aeronautics' Engineering Division. The office became the Special Devices Section in June that year and throughout World War Two it developed numerous innovative training devices. They included devices that used motion pictures to train aircraft gunners, another to train precision bombing, and a terrain modelling kit that facilitated operational planning in the field. The section grew to become the Special Devices Division and, in August 1946, it was commissioned as the Special Devices Center. Realigned several times under different organisations, in 1956 it became the Naval Training Device Center. It took on its current designation in 1993. Since the division's original creation, simulation and training have become keys to ensuring military preparedness and to adapting to new and changing roles and missions and the organisation continues to develop new and realistic training devices that support operational units. Reporting to NAWCAD, Captain Robert Betts has led the division since assuming command on May 15, 2025. ■

F-35C test aircraft CF-05 refuels from F/A-18F BuNo 165801 while conducting an advanced aerial refuelling control law test on June 26, 2018. Both aircraft were operated by Air Test and Evaluation Squadron VX-23. (US Navy/Dane Wiedmann)

May The Force Be With You

Air Test and Evaluation Squadron Two Zero (VX-20)

(Air Test and Evaluation Squadron VX-20 Insignia)

Reporting to the Naval Air Warfare Center Aircraft Division (NAWCAD) at Naval Air Station Patuxent River in Maryland, Air Test and Evaluation Squadron VX-20 conducts full spectrum developmental test and evaluation (DT&E) associated with each of the battle group support missions. These include airborne early warning (AEW), command and control (C2), anti-submarine warfare (ASW), anti-surface warfare (ASUW), electronic warfare (EW), airborne surveillance and signals intelligence (SIGINT) and strategic airborne communications. Until recently, testing of carrier onboard delivery (COD) aircraft was also assigned to VX-20. That mission transferred to NAWCAD's Air Test and Evaluation Squadron HX-21, when VX-20's Grumman C-2A was retired in March 2020. Reassignment of the COD mission to the CMV-22B version of the tiltrotor Osprey resulted in the transfer of the test mission to HX-21.

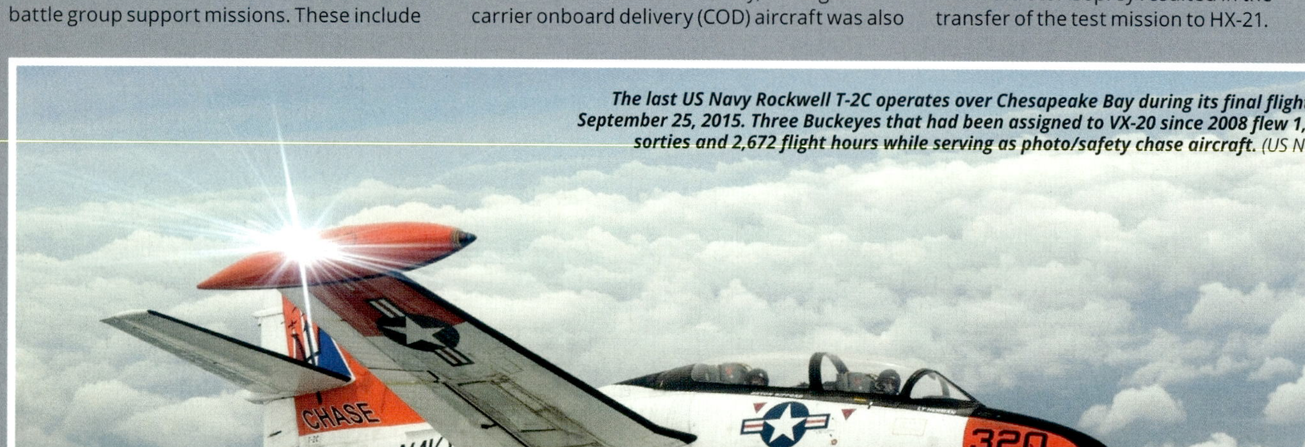

The last US Navy Rockwell T-2C operates over Chesapeake Bay during its final flight on September 25, 2015. Three Buckeyes that had been assigned to VX-20 since 2008 flew 1,978 sorties and 2,672 flight hours while serving as photo/safety chase aircraft. (US Navy)

A CH-53K assigned to VMX-1 is refuelled by KC-130T BuNo 163310 from VX-20 while transporting a retired F-35C airframe from NAS Patuxent River to the NAVAIR facility at Joint Base McGuire-Dix-Lakehurst, New Jersey, on April 24, 2024. The Lightning II was being transferred to the NAWCAD Lakehurst's Prototype, Manufacturing and Test (PMT) Department for use in future emergency recovery systems testing. (US Navy/Kyra Helwick)

US Coast Guard HC-27J serial 2712 was the first Spartan to undergo missionisation, which was carried out by the Naval Air Warfare Center Aircraft Division's AIRWorks team. The modifications installed sensors and systems designed to permit the aircraft to carry out the Coast Guard's medium range surveillance mission. The aircraft conducted its maiden flight following missionisation, on September 6, 2023. The Coast Guard has since cancelled the programme. (US Navy)

Known as 'Force', the squadron is also responsible for DT&E associated with airlift, tanker and operational support aircraft (OSA). Additionally, the squadron provides aerial refuelling for fixed-wing, rotary-wing and tiltrotor aircraft operated by its sister units HX-21 and VX-23 and safety/chase support aircraft for the squadron's own aircraft and other platforms assigned to sister squadrons within Naval Test Wing Atlantic.

The squadron supports research, development, test and evaluation (RDT&E) by providing aircraft and flight crews, maintenance services, safety oversight and facility support. It conducts flying qualities and air vehicle performance evaluations, carrier suitability, propulsion system, tactical aircraft mission system testing, weapons carriage and employment tests including compatibility and ballistic evaluations, reliability and maintainability assessments, flight fidelity simulation and flight control software development and sensor and weapons system upgrades. Additionally, VX-20 provides government flight representatives, test monitoring, chase aircraft support and facilities for contractor demonstration, validation and development work involving tactical aircraft and associated systems.

In addition to operating the largest aircraft in the naval inventory, VX-20 is tasked with testing smaller primary and intermediate training aircraft. Its fleet includes both land and carrier-based aircraft and, as a result, 'Force' conducts carrier suitability testing that involves both land-based and shipboard evaluations. Also, when required, VX-20 supports testing of US Coast Guard fixed-wing aircraft. Those efforts recently supported testing of the US Coast Guard's HC-27J Spartan, which underwent missionisation with NAWCAD's AIRWorks Team at 'Pax River'.

VX-20's inventory of more than 25 manned and unmanned aircraft currently includes the Northrop Grumman E-2D Advanced Hawkeye and MQ-4C Triton, Boeing E-6B Mercury and P-8A Poseidon, Lockheed Martin KC-130T Hercules and KC-130J Super Hercules, Beechcraft UC-12M Huron and T-6A Texan II and Gulfstream Aerospace C-38A Courier.

The squadron typically conducts more than 3,000 flight operations annually, totalling approximately 4,400 flight hours. VX-20 conducts both shore-based and shipboard carrier suitability testing. Operations take place locally at 'Pax River', Joint Base McGuire-Dix-Lakehurst in New Jersey and at sea and are supported by more than 950 sailors, marines, civilians and contractors.

VX-20 was originally established as the Antisubmarine Aircraft Test Directorate on April 1, 1975, and was a component of the US Naval Air Test Center. It was later redesignated as the Force Warfare Aircraft Test Directorate in June 1986 and was formally established as the Naval Force Aircraft Test Squadron (NAVFORAIRTESTRON) on July 21, 1995. At that time the squadron was assigned to the Commander, Naval Test Wing Atlantic at NAS Patuxent River. VX-20 assumed its current identity on May 1, 2002. The squadron has been led by Commander Jessica Barrientos since October 3, 2024. VX-20's motto, 'Full Spectrum Flight Test for the Fleet', reflects its role of testing aircraft and mission systems throughout their lifecycle. In addition to continued testing of its current fleet, the squadron will be tasked with testing of the Boeing MQ-25 Unmanned Carrier-Launched Airborne Surveillance and Strike (UCLASS) system. Testing will include ground and lab integration events, flight control system development and satellite communication testing.

Test Fleet

Serving as the US Navy's airborne command and control platform, the Northrop Grumman E-2D Advanced Hawkeye has now replaced the earlier E-2C variant in operational fleet squadrons. The E-2D first flew at Northrop Grumman's production facility in St Augustine, Florida, in August 2007. Preliminary testing was carried out from the Florida facility and the E-2D arrived at NAS Patuxent River for DT&E on May 31, 2009. ➤

ABOVE: *On loan from VMGR-452, KC-130T BuN0 164461 equipped with a NP2000 propeller system completed an aerial refuelling mission with an MV-22B during a test flight on August 24, 2020. (US Navy)*

BELOW: *Assigned the Bureau Number 169951, the first Boeing P-8A Poseidon arrived at NAS Patuxent River for testing by VX-20 on June 9, 2010. The Poseidon is one of several examples assigned to the squadron for continued testing. (US Navy/Randy Hepp)*

The squadron is currently preparing to test E-2D Delta System Software Configuration 6 (DSSC 6), which will modernise the Advanced Hawkeye's cockpit, mission computers and architecture to enhance crew effectiveness, reduce pilot workload, improve situational awareness and enable the rapid integration of new technologies through an open systems approach. DSSC 6 replaces the Advanced Hawkeye's current integrated navigation and controls and display systems and tactical mission computer and essentially results in a Block II upgrade for the aircraft. VX-20 and its predecessor organisations had operated the E-2C variant of the Hawkeye since 1971, when the first aircraft arrived at 'Pax River'. The squadron's last E-2Cs were retired in late 2019.

Testing associated with the Northrop Grumman MQ-4C Triton unmanned aircraft system began following the arrival of the first air vehicle at NAS Pax River on September 18, 2014. VX-20 has three examples of the MQ-4C on its inventory and supports an integrated test team that includes personnel from Northrop Grumman. VX-20's experience with the UAS actually began on March 28, 2006, when the first of two RQ-4A Global Hawks arrived on the base. The RQ-4As had been acquired through the Global Hawk Maritime Demonstration (GHMD) Program under the management of the Navy's UAS programme office, PMA-263. Operated by VX-20, with support from a Navy contractor integrated product team, the Global Hawks were initially used to develop the Navy's concepts of operations and tactics, techniques and procedures to support integration of the persistent unmanned intelligence, surveillance and reconnaissance (ISR) capability into the Fleet.

The Boeing E-6B Mercury TACAMO (Take Charge and Move Out) is the largest aircraft operated by the Navy and it supports the US Strategic Command serving as a survivable nuclear command and control platform. The E-6B provides a survivable communication link between the National Command Authority (NCA) and the nuclear triad that includes maned bombers, intercontinental ballistic missiles (ICBM) and submarine-launched ballistic missiles (SLBM). It first entered service under the designation E-6A in August 1989. VX-20 is responsible for one of the US Navy's 16 such aircraft. The Mercury is currently receiving several updates, including a variety of mission system obsolescence upgrades and a comprehensive service life extension programme (SLEP) designed to extend its use until at least 2040.

The E-6B is the third-generation TACAMO aircraft and follows the EC-130Q and EC-130G variants of the Hercules that first fielded the very low frequency (VLF) communications systems. Development of the VLF systems can be traced to the Naval Air Development

The prototype MQ-25 Stingray unmanned aerial vehicle refuels an E-2D over MidAmerica Airport in Mascoutah, Illinois, on August 18, 2021. The test marked the second successful refuelling flight for the MQ-25 programme. Conducted by VX-20, the flight tested the Boeing-owned MQ-25 T-1 test asset's fuel transfer, formation evaluations, wake surveys, drogue tracking and plugs at 220knots calibrated airspeed at 10,000ft. (US Navy/Boeing)

Center (NADC) in Warminster, Pennsylvania, which first tested the capability in prototype form aboard a modified Lockheed NC-121K in 1962. The NADC was renamed Naval Air Warfare Center Warminster in January 1993 and after its activities were relocated to

Boeing MQ-25 unmanned test aircraft T-1 takes off from MidAmerica Airport in Mascoutah to conduct an aerial refuelling test on June 4, 2021. Formal development test and evaluation of the Stingray will be carried out at NAS Patuxent River by VX-20. (US Navy/Boeing)

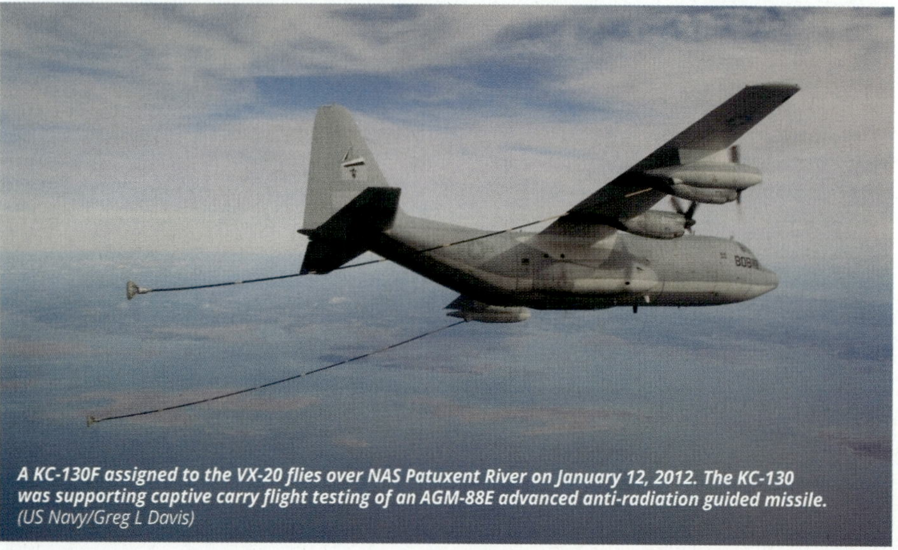

A KC-130F assigned to the VX-20 flies over NAS Patuxent River on January 12, 2012. The KC-130 was supporting captive carry flight testing of an AGM-88E advanced anti-radiation guided missile. (US Navy/Greg L Davis)

P-8A BuNo 167954 operated by VX-20 drops a Mk54 torpedo from its weapons bay during testing on February 2, 2012. *(US Navy/Greg L Davis)*

NAS Patuxent River the facility was closed in September 1996.

Previously referred to as the E-XX, the TACAMO Recapitalization Program will replace the E-6B with a new variant of the C-130J Super Hercules. Assigned the designation E-130J and the popular name Phoenix II, the new aircraft will execute the TACAMO mission when it enters service in 2028.

Development of the multi-mission maritime aircraft (MMA) began in 2004 and the first Boeing P-8A flew at Boeing Field in Seattle, Washington, on April 25, 2009. Local testing of the P-8A Poseidon began following arrival of BuNo 166951 (T1) at Pax River on April 10, 2010. The Poseidon combines the airframe of the Boeing 737-800ERX airframe with the 737-900 model's wing.

➤

Accompanied by a VX-20 P-3C, the first P-8A arrives at Pax River for testing on April 10, 2010. The Poseidon began its formal flight test programme at Boeing's Seattle facilities in October 2009. *(US Navy)*

The US Navy received more than 50 T-6As before production switched over to the T-6B variant. Texan II BuNo 165958 has served VX-20 since arriving at NAS Patuxent River on March 5, 2004. (Tom Kaminski)

In addition to testing the US Navy's P-8As, VX-20 has supported evaluations of aircraft delivered to India, Australia, the United Kingdom, Norway, Republic of Korea, New Zealand and Germany. The squadron is currently supporting testing of the Poseidon's Increment 3 Block 2 (I3B2) modifications; these provide a significant upgrade to the Poseidon, and includes new airframe racks, radome, antennas, sensors and wiring. The modification incorporates a new combat systems suite with improved computer processing, higher security architecture, a wide band satellite communication system, an ASW signals intelligence capability, a track management system and additional communications and acoustics systems that enhance search, detection and targeting capabilities.

Although operational use of the Lockheed Martin KC-130T by the US Marine Corps came to a close in April 2021, several of the aircraft remain in service with the US Navy. At least three examples have been assigned to VX-20 to support development programmes. Recent testing was conducted to certify the eight-blade NP2000 Propeller System with the KC-130T series. Envelope expansion testing that concluded in February 2025 cleared Naval Reserve KC-130Ts, equipped with the eight-blade NP2000 propeller to refuel a larger number of aircraft including the F-35B/C, F/A-18E/F, EA-18G, CH-53K, CH-47F, MH-60M/ HH-60Ws and AV-8B.

The first KC-130J aircraft arrived at NAS Patuxent River for developmental testing in September 2000. In addition to the original DT&E programme, VX-20 has tested a variety of upgrades that include the Block 8.1 cockpit updates, incorporation of the AN/AAQ-24 Large Aircraft Infrared Countermeasures (LAIRCM), the modular Harvest HAWK (Hercules Airborne Weapons Kit) system and the AN/ALQ-231 Intrepid Tiger II (IT II) electronic warfare (EW) pod capability.

A single Beechcraft UC-12M is assigned to VX-20 and serves several roles including safety, chase and photography support during test flights of other platforms. Additionally, the Huron is tasked with pilot proficiency allowing squadron pilots to maintain their flight skills. The aircraft provides logistics support

An E-2D assigned to VX-20 prepares to launch from the flight deck of the USS 'Gerald R Ford' (CVN 78) on January 27, 2020. The squadron was supporting aircraft compatibility testing of the ship's EMALS and AAG. (US Navy/MCS Jesus O Aguiar)

An E-2D and a C-2A assigned to VX-20 fly over the guided missile destroyer USS 'Zumwalt' (DDG 1000) over the Chesapeake Bay near NAS Patuxent River in Maryland as the ship transits to its new home port of San Diego, California, on October 17, 2016. (US Navy/Erik Hildebrandt)

One of two Couriers originally operated by the District of Columbia Air National Guard, C-38A 94-1570 is assigned to VX-20 and serves in a multitude of roles that include chase aircraft for flight testing, airborne radar targets and general support. The C-38A is based on the Israel Aircraft Industries Astra SPX airframe. (US Navy/Stephen Wolff)

transporting light cargo and personnel in the operational support airlift (OSA) role.

The Beechcraft T-6A Texan II has supported testing since March 5, 2004, when BuNo 165958 arrived. The squadron's T-6A was in fact the first production Texan II and was transferred from the USAF and was assigned serial 95-3001. Like the other aircraft on the squadron's inventory, the T-6A supports testing of upgrades to the US Navy's trainer fleet. Additionally, it serves other roles including chase and pilot proficiency.

Based on the Israel Aircraft Industries (IAI) Model 1125A Astra/Gulfstream Aerospace G100 corporate jet, two C-38A Couriers were originally operated by the District of Columbia Air National Guard's 201st Airlift Squadron prior to their transfer to VX-20 in 2015. They replaced a number of Rockwell T-2C Buckeye trainers that had served in that role until retired on September 25, 2015. In addition to serving a chase platform, the Couriers act as radar test targets, support pilot proficiency and air transport.

Boeing was selected as the winner of the Unmanned Carrier-Launched Airborne Surveillance and Strike (UCLASS) programme on August 30, 2018, and ordered four aircraft, which received the designation MQ-25A and popular name Stingray. Three additional test MQ-25As were ordered on April 2, 2020. The Stingray will be the world's first operational, carrier-based unmanned aircraft and provide aerial refuelling and intelligence, surveillance and reconnaissance (ISR) capabilities intended to enhance capability and versatility for the carrier air wing (CVW) and carrier strike group (CSG). Stingray's two major segments comprise the MQ-25 Air System (air vehicle), and the Unmanned Carrier Aviation Mission Control System (UMCS).

Boeing's company-owned prototype MQ-25 first flew on September 19, 2019, from MidAmerica St Louis Airport in Mascoutah, Illinois. During summer 2021, the MQ-25 T1 test asset successfully conducted aerial refuelling test flights with the F/A-18F, F-35C and E-2D. Although testing has been carried out from the Illinois facility adjacent to Scott Air Force Base, once the first production-representative Stingray flies, testing will transition to NAS Patuxent River with VX-20 taking charge. ■

P-8A BuNo 167954 successfully launches the first Mk54 exercise torpedo during testing on October 13, 2011. The test was intended to verify safe separation of the lightweight torpedo from the Poseidon. The P-8A can carry up to five Mk54s in its internal weapons bay. (US Navy/Liz Wolter)

Arrival of VX-20's T-6A was marked on March 5, 2004, when BuNo 165958 arrived at NAS Patuxent River. The Texan II was developed for the US Air Force and Navy under the Joint Primary Aircraft Training System (JPATS) programme. (US Navy/James Darcy)

The first E-2D Advanced Hawkeye prepares to refuel from a Boeing 707 operated by Omega Tanker above NAS Patuxent River, Maryland, during a test flight. (US Navy)

Blackjacks Deliver a Winning Hand

Air Test and Evaluation Squadron Two One (HX-21)

Nicknamed the 'Blackjacks', air test and evaluation squadron HX-21 conducts research, development, test and evaluation (RDT&E) of rotary-wing and tiltrotor aircraft for the US Navy, Marine Corps and Coast Guard. The aircraft are assigned to a variety of missions, including anti-submarine warfare (ASW), anti-surface warfare (ASUW), light attack, light, medium and heavy transport, carrier onboard delivery (COD), search and rescue, combat search and rescue (CSAR), naval special warfare (NSW), airborne mine countermeasures (AMCM), training and general support. Evaluations are carried out on the aircraft, airborne sensors and weapons systems. HX-21 is one of three test squadrons aligned under the Naval Air Warfare Center Aircraft Division (NAWC-AD) at Naval Air Station (NAS) Patuxent River, Maryland, and reports to the Commander, Naval Test Wing Atlantic.

The squadron traces its history to the establishment of the rotary-wing section of the Naval Air Test Center's (NATC) Flight Test Division at NAS Patuxent River, on April 25, 1949. Named the Rotary Wing Test Directorate on April 1, 1975, it became the Naval Rotary Wing Aircraft Test Directorate in July 1986. Elevation to squadron-level

followed on July 21, 1995, when it was formally established as the Naval Rotary Wing Aircraft Test Squadron (NAVRWAIRTESTRON). At that time, it was assigned to the Commander, Naval Test Wing Atlantic at NAS Patuxent River. HX-21 assumed its current identity on May 1, 2002.

The squadron operates a varied fleet of aircraft in ten different type/model/series (TMS). The inventory includes the Bell UH-1Y, AH-1Z and TH-57C, Bell-Boeing MV-22B and CMV-22B, Sikorsky MH-60R/S, CH-53E/K and VH-92A. The squadron also supports NAS Patuxent River's search and rescue (SAR) division, which operates several

TH-57C BuNo 162013 operates near NAS Patuxent River on February 27, 2019. The Sea Ranger is one of three examples operated by HX-21 as support aircraft. (Mike Wilson)

A UH-1Y from HX-21 returns to NAS Patuxent River after completing the first test flight with a developmental electronic warfare pod on June 8, 2015. US Navy A UH-1Y from HX-21 returns to NAS Patuxent River after completing the first test flight with a developmental electronic warfare pod on June 8, 2015. (US Navy)

(Air Test and Evaluation Squadron HX-21 Insignia)

The UH-1Y Venom made its first shipboard landing on May 7, 2005, on the Multipurpose Amphibious Assault Ship USS 'Bataan' (LHD-5) off the Virginia Capes, while undergoing development test and evaluation. *(US Navy/Troy Lancaster)*

MH-60S Seahawks. The 'SAR Dogs' provide 24/7 search and rescue services, responding to various emergencies, including boater distress, medical evacuations and assisting other agencies such as the Coast Guard. The highly trained team frequently undergoes evaluations to maintain readiness and proficiency in life-saving operations. Those assigned to HX-21 include active-duty US Navy and Marine Corps officers and enlisted personnel, civilian employees and a large number of contractor personnel. Operating from Hangars 109 and 111, HX-21's ramp is shared with the US Naval Air Test Pilot School and is adjacent to the air station's former seaplane ramp.

The squadron's tasks include developmental flight tests, aircraft compatibility and dynamic interface testing and envelope expansion. Flight testing of rotary-wing aircraft includes launch and recovery, rotor start and shutdown, blade fold. In addition to traditional RDT&E, HX-21 conducts sea trials for rotorcraft that ▶

An MH-60S Seahawk operated by HX-21 fires a 2.75in rocket during a weapons test near NAS Patuxent River, Maryland. *(US Navy/Erik Hildebrandt)*

The first CMV-22B lands at NAS 'Pax River' on February 2, 2020, after completing a ferry flight from Bell's Amarillo Assembly Center in Texas. The carrier onboard delivery variant of the Osprey is replacing the Northrop Grumman C-2A in the COD role. (US Navy)

will operate from US Navy ships or those of international partner nations. Those vessels range in size from large deck aircraft carriers and amphibious assault ships to smaller amphibious ships, destroyers, littoral combat ships and US Coast Guard cutters.

Sea trials comprise a series of tests that evaluate the performance of the aircraft at sea. Shipboard compatibility testing includes towing the aircraft around the deck and in the hangar, performing maintenance while aboard the ship, ensuring the aircraft fits in all the locations it needs to around the ship deck and hangar and evaluating chain/tie-down procedures. Flight testing of rotary-wing aircraft includes launch and recovery, rotor start and shutdown, blade fold. HX-21 is tasked to conduct dynamic interface (DI) ship-air test trials that evaluate and confirm the safe launch and recovery envelope's safe operating parameters for shipboard operations.

DI defines the operational limits that are known as SHOL – ship-helicopter operating limits – for rotorcraft landing on or taking off from moving, pitching and rolling ship decks under a turbulent 'ship air-wake'. Before the aircraft can deploy operationally aboard any specific type or class of ship, they must undergo DI testing. Shipboard compatibility testing is conducted at increasing wind speed and varying wind directions relative to the aircraft.

Not limited to US Navy ships, in November 2023, HX-21's V-22 test team conducted an extensive series of DI ship-air test trials aboard the Royal Navy Queen Elizabeth-class aircraft carrier HMS *Prince of Wales* (R09). Over the course of several weeks the V-22 team's test pilots and flight test engineers significantly expanded the Osprey's operational envelope aboard the ship. Operations included a variety of landings, take-offs and deck operations, as well as ground handling and hangar operations. The trials marked a major milestone in the integration of maritime forces between the US and UK.

US Marine Corps Colonel Aaron Okun assumed command of HX-21 at NAS Patuxent River on February 13, 2025. Previously, he had served as HX-21's chief test pilot.

Test Fleet

Formally retired from training duties on September 19, 2025, Bell TH-57C Sea Ranger continues to serve with the 'Blackjacks'. HX-21 uses the TH-57C for a variety of duties including photo and chase support, utility missions and general 'readiness flights' that include pilot proficiency and currency. The squadron recently received a third TH-57C following the type's retirement from training duties.

Known as the Venom, the first of two Bell UH-1Y prototypes initially flew with the H-1 Upgrades Integrated Test Team (ITT) at NAS Patuxent River on July 3, 2002. Developed alongside the AH-1Z under the H-1 Upgrades programme, beginning in 1996, the Venom replaced the earlier UH-1N Twin Huey in service with the Marine Corps.

The first of three AH-1Z prototypes arrived at 'Pax River' in April 2001 after completing the first phase of development testing at Bell Helicopter Textron's facility in Arlington, Texas, where it accumulated almost 60 flight hours.

Developmental testing was completed in early 2006. Continued upgrades to the two platforms recently added additional capabilities, including a digital interoperability suite that added Link 16 and ANW2 data links and a gateway to share information across various networks. New weapons capabilities enable both helicopters to deploy the AGM-179A joint air-to-ground missile (JAGM). It is a dual-mode, air-to-surface precision missile with semi-active laser and millimetre-wave radar seekers that provide

The third engineering development model (EDM-3) CH-53K conducts refuelling trials with a KC-130J over Chesapeake Bay on April 6, 2020. Assigned BuNo 168781, the King Stallion was conducting aerial refuelling wake testing with the Super Hercules. (US Navy)

MV-22B 166494 assigned to HX-21 conducts sea trials aboard the Royal Navy aircraft carrier HMS 'Prince of Wales' (R09), which was operating in the eastern Atlantic Ocean on January 24, 2024. (Brad Renninger)

'fire-and-forget' capability against both land and maritime targets.

Developed by a team comprising Bell Helicopter and Boeing beginning in May 1986, the V-22 series has been undergoing testing at NAS Patuxent River since the first of six full-scale development (FSD) V-22As flew in March 1989. The Osprey suffered through a long-developmental period that led to several major changes and numerous redesign efforts. Now fully fielded by the US Marine Corps, testing of upgrades to the MV-22B continues at Pax River.

The first of two US Navy CMV-22Bs arrived there after completing its ferry flight from Bell's Amarillo Assembly Center in Texas on February 2, 2020. The carrier onboard delivery variant of the Osprey had conducted its first flight in Amarillo in December 2019.

Because it was based on the MV-22B, developmental testing was focused on its unique mission requirements and systems and included data collection on fuel and structural loads, and integration of its beyond line-of-sight radio and improved lighting systems. The CMV-22B formally achieved initial operational capability (IOC) on December 14, 2021. ▶

A CH-53K operated by HX-21 lands at Naval Air Station Key West's Boca Chica Field on May 15, 2020. The King Stallion was evaluating several structural modifications that were developed to correct issues discovered during developmental flight tests. (US Navy/Danette Baso Silvers)

Aircraft assigned to Air Test and Evaluation Squadron HX-21 prepare to lift off from NAS Patuxent River, Maryland, at the start of a squadron-wide formation flight on March 25, 2022. The flight highlighted the variety of rotary-wing and tiltrotor aircraft flown and tested by HX-21 test pilots and flight test engineers. The mixed formation included examples of the CMV-22B, MH-60R, MH-60S, UH-1Y, AH-1Z, VH-92A and MV-22B. (US Navy/Lt Ben Putbrese)

MV-22B BuNo 166491 lifts off from NAS 'Pax River' during a successful biofuel test flight on August 10, 2011. During the test mission, the HX-21-assigned Osprey flew at altitudes of up to 25,000ft on a 50-50 blend of camelina-based biofuel and standard petroleum-based JP-5 fuel. (US Navy/Steven Kays)

An MH-60S Seahawk operated by HX-21 fires an AGM-114 Hellfire air-to-ground missile during a weapons test near NAS Patuxent River. (US Navy)

Initially assigned the designation CH-60S, the Sikorsky MH-60S Seahawk was first delivered to the Rotary Wing Aircraft Test Squadron when the second production, 'Sierra', arrived on May 15, 2000. Originally known as the SH-60R, the 'Romeo' variant of the Sea King first arrived at Pax River for testing in 2001. Both variants of the Seahawk have received significant upgrades to their systems and weapons since they were deployed operationally and HX-21 continues to conduct developmental testing of upgrades for the MH-60R and MH-60S.

Flight testing of the YCH-53E prototype began at Pax River in August 1976. The Super Stallion was developed as a more capable replacement for the earlier CH-53A/D versions of the Sea Stallion. Evaluations of limited upgrades continue as the Marine Corps prepares to sunset its primary heavy-lift helicopter.

HX-21 received its first CH-53K King Stallion helicopter from Sikorsky on June 30, 2017. The Engineering Development and Manufacturing Model was flown from Sikorsky's facility in Florida to Pax River. The squadron eventually received four CH-53K EDM models and the King Stallion first went to sea aboard the amphibious assault ship USS *Wasp* (LHD 1) for initial sea trials in June 2020. The CH-53K completed a second at-sea period over five full days and nights aboard the San Antonio-class amphibious transport dock USS *Arlington* (LPD 24) in the Atlantic Ocean in March 2023. Supported by Marine Operational Test and Evaluation Squadron HMX-1 and Marine Heavy Helicopter Squadron HMH-461, the tests primarily involved envelope expansion testing. Tests performed during the event included launch and recovery, rotor start and shutdown, blade fold, and shipboard compatibility testing.

Test and evaluation of the Sikorsky VH-92A is conducted by the Presidential Helicopter Test Team, which is a collaborative effort between HX-21 and Marine Helicopter Squadron HMX-1. Known as the Patriot, the VH-92A is based on Sikorsky's model S-92A commercial helicopter. The first VH-92A Engineering Development Model (EDM) aircraft arrived at Pax River on August 2, 2018.

Earlier, the first flight of EDM-1 was at Sikorsky's facility in Stratford, Connecticut, on July 28, 2017. The initial pair of EDM Patriots will remain assigned to HX-21 to support testing throughout the helicopter's time in service with HMX-1.

HX-21 and its predecessor organisations have supported the presidential and VIP rotary-wing airlift missions since 1957, testing all aircraft that have flown under the callsign 'Marine One'; they include the VH-34, VH-3A/D, VH-60N, MV-22B and VH-92A.

Work associated with the VH-92A is carried out at the Presidential Helicopter Support Facility (PHSF) at Pax River. The dedicated, secure facility was built specifically for presidential helicopter support and includes a hangar, laboratories and assembly areas.

The 202,000sq ft PHSF, which was constructed at a cost of $84.5m and completed in 2006, added a new hangar, apron and support buildings. This secure facility also houses technical laboratories, maintenance areas and offices specifically

A CMV-22B from Air Test and Evaluation Squadron HX-21 leads a flight of aircraft representing each of the types flown by the 'Blackjacks' on March 25, 2022. The mixed formation included examples of the CMV-22B, MH-60R, MH-60S, UH-1Y, AH-1Z, VH-92A and MV-22B. (US Navy/Lt Ben Putbrese)

Retired in October 2020, NVH-3A BuNo 150614 served as a test bed for modifications associated with the US Marine Corps' Presidential Helicopter Fleet for more than 30 years. *(US Navy)*

dedicated to supporting the presidential helicopter programme. It is designed to handle the unique requirements of maintaining and supporting the helicopters used for presidential transport. This includes tasks like maintenance, repairs and modifications, ensuring the aircraft are ready for their critical role. Development efforts associated with the mission fall under the Presidential Helicopters Program PMA-274. ∎

Developmental testing of a new Sikorsky VH-92A presidential helicopter was carried out at NAS Patuxent River by HX-21. Based on Sikorsky's successful civil S-92A, the Patriot will soon replace the Sikorsky VH-3D in its role as 'Marine One'. *(US Navy)*

One of three prototype AH-1Z Vipers is prepared for a mission at NAS Patuxent River on July 6, 2004. The Viper was developed by Bell Helicopter under the H-1 upgrades programme. *(Tom Kaminski)*

Reaching Higher

Air Test and Evaluation Squadron Two Three (VX-23)

Based at Naval Air Station Patuxent River, Maryland, Air Test and Evaluation Squadron VX-23 is the US Navy's fixed-wing tactical aircraft test squadron. Known as the 'Salty Dogs', the service's largest test squadron is a component of the Naval Air Warfare Center Aircraft Division (NAWC-AD) and is responsible for more than 40 aircraft that support around 200 test projects.

Often referred to as Strike Test, the squadron supports the research, development, test and evaluation (RDT&E) by providing aircraft and flight crews, maintenance services, safety oversight and facility support. It carries out flying qualities and performance evaluations, shipboard suitability, propulsion system testing, tactical aircraft mission system testing, ordnance compatibility and ballistic efforts, reliability and maintainability assessments, flight fidelity simulation and flight control software development. Additionally, VX-23 provides government flight representatives, test monitoring, chase aircraft support and facilities for contractor demonstration, validation and development work involving tactical aircraft and associated systems.

The squadron's workforce comprises officers from the US Navy, Marine Corps and international air arms, as well as US Navy and Marine Corps enlisted personnel, civilians, employees and contractors. In addition to test pilots, the personnel provide aircraft maintenance and test planning and conduct safety oversight and support for the squadron's aircraft.

The squadron typically conducts more than 3,000 flight operations annually, totalling around 4,400 flight hours. VX-23 conducts both shore-based and shipboard carrier suitability testing. Shore-based testing is conducted at numerous sites including locally at Patuxent River and at Joint Base McGuire-Dix-Lakehurst, New Jersey.

VX-23 was originally known as the Naval Strike Aircraft Test Directorate when it was established as a component of the Naval Air Test Center on April 1, 1975. However, its history can be traced to the establishment of the Naval Air Test Center and its Flight Test Division on June 16, 1945. Elevated to squadron status on July 21, 1995, it was designated as the Naval Strike Aircraft Test Squadron (NAVSTRKAIRTESTRON) and assigned to the Commander, Naval Test Wing Atlantic at NAS Patuxent River the same day.

The squadron currently operates seven different fixed-wing strike, electronic attack and strike training aircraft – the Boeing F/A-18D Hornet, F/A-18E, F/A-18F Super Hornet, EA-18G Growler, T-45C Goshawk and Lockheed Martin F-35B and F-35C Lightning II.

VX-23 operates and maintains NAWCAD's TC-7 steam catapult and arresting gear facility, which has a TC-7 catapult, Mk 7 arresting gear unit, associated visual landing aids and an AN/SPN-46 automated carrier landing system (ACLS). Capable of launching aircraft weighing as much as 85,000lb (38,555kg), the catapult has been operational since 1954 while the arresting gear

F-35B test aircraft BF-03 from VX-23 conducts flight tests carrying the AGM-158C long-range anti-ship missile (LRASM) over NAS Patuxent River on September 9, 2024. The certification flight was part of ongoing integration efforts, conducted by the F-35 Integrated Test Force team. The initial test flights were intended to evaluate flutter, loads and flying qualities with two AGM-158s loaded on external stations. (US Navy/Dane Wiedmann)

VX-23 assigned F/A-18F BuNo 169125 performs a touch-and-go landing at Atlantic City International Airport in Pomona, New Jersey, on July 5, 2017. (US Air National Guard/MSgt Matt Hecht)

F-35C test aircraft CF-02 lifts off from NAS Patuxent River, Maryland, at the start of the Lightning II's final system development and demonstration (SDD) flight at NAS Pax River on April 11, 2018. The mission collected loads data while carrying external 2,000lb GBU-31 joint direct attack munitions (JDAM) and AIM-9X Sidewinder heat-seeking missiles. (US Navy)

was first used in 1961 and is capable of stopping a 50,000lb (2,2679kg) aircraft at a 130knot (241km/h) engagement speed. The facility evaluates an aircraft's suitability for carrier operations and allows the aircraft to be launched and recovered under a variety of configurations without the danger of actually operating at sea.

Similar to systems first used aboard USS Forrestal-class 'super carriers', the TC-7 first entered service at Pax River in 1954. The system underwent a $1.6million modernisation project in 1986, received another major upgrade in 1993 and has undergone continuous upgrades since then. Driven by a linear piston-type steam engine, the site is considered the Navy's premier aircraft carrier suitability test facility.

Testing associated with the joint strike fighter (JSF) programme saw several new facilities constructed at Pax River. Built specifically to support the JSF programme, a hover pit facility was completed in late 2000. Designed to emulate an 'out-of-ground-effect' environment, it was first used to test the Boeing X-32B as part of short-take-off and vertical-landing (STOVL) testing.

Designed to replicate the runway of an aircraft carrier, the land-based ski jump was the first of its type to be built anywhere in the world. It was constructed to enable the F-35B to conduct ramp-assisted short take-off testing on land before making the first shipboard ski jump launch from the Royal Navy aircraft carrier HMS *Queen Elizabeth*. Carried out by a joint US-UK team, the land-based testing demonstrated the aircraft's ability to safely take-off and land. First used in June 2015 by the F-35B, VX-23 later conducted ski jump take-off tests with an F/A-18E in December 2020.

It is also responsible for the certification of nuclear aircraft carrier and amphibious ▶

(Air Test and Evaluation Squadron VX-23 Insignia)

An EA-18G from Air Test and Evaluation Squadron VX-23 awaits its next flight aboard the aircraft carrier USS 'Gerald R Ford' (CVN 78) on January 28, 2020. The Growler was supporting aircraft compatibility testing associated with the ship's electromagnetic aircraft launch system (EMALS) and advanced arresting gear (AAG). (US Navy/MCS Jesus O Aguiar)

A pair of EA-18Gs assigned to Air Test and Evaluation Squadron VX-23 fly in formation over the Atlantic Ocean on August 15, 2018. Assigned BuNos 169143 and 168377, the aircraft were the 134th and 63rd Growlers produced by Boeing. (US Navy)

Air Test and Evaluation Squadron VX-23 supported F-35B sea trials aboard the Italian Navy aircraft carrier ITS 'Cavour' (CVH 550) off of the east coast of the US during March 2021. F-35B BuNo 168717 operated over the western Atlantic Ocean near the carrier on March 1. The sea trials were intended to clear the Italian Navy to operate its Lightning IIs from the ship. (US Navy)

F-35C test aircraft CF-05 makes its approach to land on USS 'Nimitz' (CVN 68) on November 3, 2014. Conducted as part of the F-35C's sea trials, the landing was part of the aircraft's 91st flight.
Lockheed Martin/Andy Wolfe

F-35C test aircraft CF-03 conducts the initial arrested landing aboard the aircraft carrier USS 'Nimitz' (CVN 68) on November 3, 2014. Conducted as part of the F-35C's sea trials, the landing was carried out during the aircraft's 182nd flight. (US Navy/ Alexander H Groves)

assault ship fight decks, as well as precision systems such as the joint precision approach and landing system (JPALS) and the traditional optical landing system (OLS). Developed by Raytheon, JPALS is a software-based GPS navigation system that provides all-weather navigation and guidance for aircraft to land on aircraft carriers and amphibious assault ships, regardless of weather or sea conditions. Deployed on all US Navy aircraft carriers and amphibious assault ships, and international vessels such as the UK Royal Navy's two HMS Queen Elizabeth-class aircraft carriers and Italy's ITS *Cavour*, JPALS uses an encrypted datalink to connect with GPS sensors and antennas on the aircraft and the

F-35B BuNo 168717 makes its final approach to land aboard the Italian aircraft carrier ITS 'Cavour' (CVH 550), while test aircraft BF-05 remans chained to the flight deck. Operated by Air Test and Evaluation Squadron VX-23, the Lightning IIs were conducting day envelope expansion test flights as part of sea trials. (US Navy/Wiedmann)

F/A-18D BuNo 161356 assigned to Air Test and Evaluation Squadron VX-23 makes a full afterburner take-off from Pax River on December 16, 2011. The legacy Hornet was serving as a chase aircraft in support of F-35 testing. (US Navy/Greg L Davis)

Flown by a UK Royal Navy test pilot assigned to VX-23 and the Lightning II Integrated Test team, F-35C test aircraft CF-02 conducts an aerial refuelling test with KC-130T BuNo 162309, operated by VX-20 on February 24, 2021. (US Navy)

ship. The OLS is a visual-based aid and uses a series of coloured lights and lenses to provide pilots with a visual reference of their glide path during landing.

Flight deck certification involves the testing and evaluation of fixed-wing tactical aircraft and their systems to ensure the aircraft can safely launch and recover in the maritime environment. The certification verifies that a ship and its crew are ready to carry out air operations by evaluating the flight deck's ability to function under operational conditions and the crew's capability to manage flight operations.

VX-23 has been under the command of Commander Eric Zilberman since June 12, 2025.

Test Fleet

VX-23 and predecessor organisations have operated a varied fleet of aircraft. However, as the number of different platforms deployed by the US Navy has been reduced, that variety has given way to just a handful of different aircraft assigned to the squadron.

Testing of the McDonnell Douglas, now Boeing F/A-18 Hornet series began at NAS Patuxent River following the arrival of the first two-seat TF-18A on December 17, 1978. The first single-seat F/A-18A followed on January 16, 1979. In total, 11 developmental Hornets underwent testing at NAS Pax River before the first production jets arrived. Since then, VX-23 has tested all seven platforms based on the airframe – the F/A-18A, F/A-18B, F/A-18C and F/A-18D Hornet, F/A-18E and F/A-18F Super Hornet and the EA-18G Growler.

Testing of Hornet, Super Hornet and Growler aircraft for international customers including Australia, Finland, Kuwait, Spain and Switzerland has also been supported by VX-23. The legacy Hornet is now the longest-serving type operated by the 'Salty Dogs'. The first F/A-18E/F Super Hornet flight test aircraft arrived at NAS Patuxent River on February 15, 1996 and the last of the seven development jets touched down on February 1, 1997. Testing of the Block III Super Hornet began ▶

NF/A-18D BuNo 163986 from VX-23 flies in formation with a French Navy Rafale F3 fighter from the French Naval Aeronautics Experimentation Center (CEPA/10S) on April 28, 2025. A joint test team was conducting flight tests that enabled the French fighter to aerial refuel US Navy Super Hornets EA-18G Growlers. The tanker qualification partnership was intended to pave the way for an extended reach and enhanced interoperability for allied airpower. (US Navy/Erik Hildebrandt)

during the summer of 2020 and the first new-build F/A-18F was delivered to the squadron on August 31, 2021.

The first EA-18G Growler developmental test aircraft arrived at NAS Pax River on September 22, 2006; prior to its arrival, the squadron had conducted tests with one of the developmental F/A-18Fs that had been modified as an aerodynamic test platform. Recent test programmes for the Super Hornet and Growler have involved evaluating and clearing the former to deploy new weapons and next-generation jammer mid-band pods for the latter.

Testing of the Lightning II can be traced to February 2001, when the Lockheed Martin X-35C joint strike fighter prototype first arrived at Pax River. Initially flown at Palmdale, California, on December 16, 2000, evaluation of the carrier variant concluded in March 2001. The X-35C logged 73 flights and 252 field carrier-landing practises at the Maryland base.

The first F-35B arrived at NAS Patuxent River on November 15, 2009. Designated as BF-1, it was the first of four developmental aircraft deployed for test and evaluation. Production aircraft deliveries followed on October 4, 2012, when BuNo 168313 touched down. The F-35B went to sea for the first time aboard the amphibious assault ship USS *Wasp* (LHD 4) in support of the Developmental Testing I (DT-I) period in October 2011. Also conducted aboard the USS *Wasp*, DT-II followed in August 2013.

Shipboard evaluation concluded following operations aboard the amphibious assault ship USS *America* (LHA 6) during DT-III in November 2016.

Besides the aircraft destined for service with the US Marine Corps, VX-23 also supported testing of F-35Bs from the UK and Italy. Special facilities constructed at Pax River to support F-35B testing included the ski jump that simulated the flight decks of the Royal Navy and Italian Navy aircraft carriers and their ramp-assisted short take-off (STO). The hover pit that was originally constructed for the joint strike fighter competition supported hover and vertical landing evaluations.

The arrival of the first Italian Navy F-35B serial (AL-1) from Cameri Air Base near Milan occurred on January 31, 2018 and marked the first transatlantic crossing for the F-35B.

The F-35 Pax River Integrated Test Force (ITF) conducted the First of Class Flight Trials (FOCFTs) aboard the UK Royal Navy's aircraft carrier, HMS *Queen Elizabeth* in October 2018. Similar tests followed on the Italian aircraft carrier ITS *Cavour* in March 2021 and the HMS *Prince of Wales* (R09) in 2023.

One of two T-45C assigned to Air Test and Evaluation Squadron VX-23, makes its final approach to an arrested landing on the flight deck of aircraft carrier USS 'Gerald R Ford' (CVN 78) on January 17, 2020. BuNo 163635 was supporting aircraft compatibility testing of the ship's electromagnetic aircraft launch systems (EMALS) and advanced arresting gear (AAG). (US Navy/MC2 Ruben Reed)

Northrop Grumman X-47B BuNo 168064 (AV-2) lands at Pax River, Maryland, at the conclusion of the 100th flight conducted under the US Navy's Unmanned Combat Air System Demonstration (UCAS-D) programme on September 18, 2016. The X-47B completed all objectives for the carrier phase for the UCAS-D programme, including three at-sea periods over eight months. It conducted a total of 16 precision approaches to the carrier flight deck, including five planned wave-offs, nine touch-and-go landings, two arrested landings and three catapult launches. (US Navy)

T-45C BuNo 165080, assigned to thVX-23 'Salty Dogs' conducts a test flight from NAS Patuxent River, Maryland using a biofuel blend of JP-5 jet fuel and plant-based camelina on August 24, 2011. The Goshawk is one of two assigned to the 'Salty Dogs'. (US Navy/Kelly Schindler)

Assigned BuNo 166641, the first F/A-18F was modified to serve as an aerodynamic prototype for the EA-18G Growler and was assigned to the NAWCAD for testing. It was later assigned the designation NEA-18G reflecting its status as permanent test asset. (US Navy)

An F/A-18E conducts an advanced aerial refuelling control law test with an F-35C over NAS Patuxent River on June 26, 2018. The Super Hornet and Lightning II were both assigned to VX-23. (US Navy/Dane Wiedmann)

More recently, VX-23 and the F-35 ITF conducted developmental sea trials aboard the Japan Maritime Self-Defense Force Izumo-class multi-functional destroyer JS *Kaga* (DDH-184) in 2024. The flights were intended to gather the necessary data to certify F-35B operations from the JMSDF's largest ship.

The first F-35C carrier variant arrived at NAS Patuxent River on November 6, 2010. In preparation for actual testing at sea, F-35C test aircraft CF-3 made the first TC-7 catapult launch at Pax River on November 4, 2011.

Previous catapult testing was conducted at Joint Base McGuire-Dix Lakehurst in New Jersey. The F-35C's first arrested carrier landing was on November 3, 2014, aboard the aircraft carrier USS *Nimitz* (CVN 68). This landing was conducted as part of the F-35C's initial at-sea DT-I period. The squadron subsequently conducted DT-II in October 2015, aboard the USS *Dwight D Eisenhower* (CVN 69). A third period of at-sea testing under DT-III was carried out on the USS *George Washington* (CVN 73) in August 2016.

Testing of the F-35B and F-35C continues in support of Technology Refresh 3 (TR-3) and Block 4. The TR-3 provides hardware and software upgrades that are required for the Block 4 updates. They include increased processing power and memory, enhanced displays and open architecture. In addition to new weapons, sensors and electronic warfare capabilities, Block 4 integrates new and enhanced munitions for aircraft including the AIM-260 joint advanced tactical missile (JATM), the GBU-53/B StormBreaker small diameter bomb (SDB), AGM-88G advanced anti-radiation guided missile-extended range (AARGM-ER) and a new weapons rack that increases internal weapons capacity. The new rack will enable the F-35 to carry more ordnance internally while retaining its stealth capabilities.

While DT&E for smaller propeller-driven trainer aircraft is aligned under VX-20, those efforts for jet-powered trainers are assigned to VX-23. Developed by McDonnell Douglas under the US Navy's VTXTS advanced trainer programme, the initial T-45A flew on April 16, 1988 and the first Goshawk was delivered to NAS Patuxent River on October 10, 1990; the second followed on November 15. VX-23 has operated the T-45C variant since the first example with the Cockpit-21 upgrades arrived in October 1997. Ongoing testing continues to support the programme as upgrades are made to the carrier-capable advanced training aircraft. The service recently began the search for a replacement for the T-45C. Unlike the Goshawk, the new trainer will not be a carrier-capable aircraft. ■

Assigned to Air Test and Evaluation Squadron VX-23, F/A-18F BuNo 166969 flies over the aircraft carrier USS 'Gerald R Ford' (CVN 78) on July 28, 2017. The aircraft was supporting test and evaluation operations. (US Navy/Erik Hildebrandt)

Operating from the Webster Naval Outlying Field (NOLF) in St Inigoes, Maryland, Air Test and Evaluation Squadron UX-24 is the US Navy's only dedicated unmanned air system (UAS) test unit. Reporting to the Naval Air Warfare Center Aircraft Division (NAWC-AD) via the Naval Test Wing Atlantic, the 'Ghost Wolves' currently provides research, development, test and evaluation (RDT&E) services for Group 1-5 UAS, including the Boeing Insitu RQ-21A Blackjack, Navmar Applied Sciences Corporation (NASC) RQ-23A Tigershark, Aeronautics RQ-26A Aerostar and General Atomics MQ-9A Reaper.

Located near the mouth of the Potomac River, 15 miles south of Naval Air Station Patuxent River, the Webster NOLF, which is also known as the NAWCAD Webster Field Annex, covers around 1,000 acres. Featuring two 5,000ft runways, the installation's unique facilities direct entry into restricted operating areas, exclusive-use areas available for small UAS, a dedicated UAS operations centre and proximity to waterways for maritime operations. The Webster NOLF was originally commissioned in October 1943.

In addition to its current responsibilities, the squadron will also support testing associated with the Boeing MQ-25A Stingray when the first air vehicles arrive at NAS Patuxent River in 2026. On November 5, 2024, UX-24 used the General Atomics MD-5 Ground Control Station (GCS) at 'Pax River' to command and control a jet-powered General Atomics MQ-20 UAS. The Avenger was serving as a surrogate for the MQ-25A and operated from the contractor's Desert Horizon flight operations facility in El Mirage, California. The demonstration was part of an effort intended to advance technology for future collaborative combat aircraft (CCA).

In early 2025, the squadron successfully integrated the first SkyTower II pod with an MQ-9A Reaper UAS. The airborne network extension pod enhances cross-domain communication capabilities and links communications between disparate forces.

The squadron also continues to test of a number of smaller commercial unmanned systems that can support a variety of missions including logistics and intelligence, surveillance and reconnaissance (ISR). Originally known as the Unmanned Aircraft Systems Test Directorate (UASTD), UX-24 was formally established on October 1, 2018. Commander Tyler Hurst has led UX-24 since July 11, 2024.

Test Fleet

Until the last examples were divested in March 2023, the Boeing Insitu RQ-21A Blackjack provided the US Marine Corps with an expeditionary UAS capability. The twin-boom, single-engine small tactical unmanned aircraft system (STUAS) is powered by an 8hp electronic fuel-injected (EFI) reciprocating piston engine, weighs 134lb (61kg) and has an endurance of 16 hours. The Group 3 expeditionary UAS is operated from a pneumatic launcher and a recovery system known as Skyhook, allowing deployments from land or at sea. Although first flown on February 19, 2013, testing began at Webster Field on June 12 that year.

Known as the TigerShark, the RQ-23A was developed in the early 2000s as a Group 3 Medium Altitude Long Endurance (MALE) multi-purpose unmanned aerial vehicle (UAV) by Navmar Applied Sciences Corporation (NASC). The TigerShark is launched and recovered

(Air Test and Evaluation Squadron UX-24 Insignia)

An unmanned RQ-23A taxies during a test mission at NAS Patuxent River's Navy Webster Naval Outlying Field in St Inigoes. Also known as the Webster Field Annex, the airfield is the home of the NAWCADs UX-24 'Ghost Wolves'. (US Navy)

Webster Field's Ghost Wolves

Air Test and Evaluation Squadron Two Four (UX-24)

MQ-9A BuNo 170717 operated by UX-24 conducts an advanced payload integration test with the SkyTower II airborne network-extension and Reaper Defense Electronic Support System/Scalable Open Architecture Reconnaissance (RDESS/SOAR) pods under its left and right wings. *(US Navy)*

A Northrop Grumman MQ-8C Fire Scout unmanned helicopter conducts a flight test at NAS Patuxent River's Webster Field Annex in St Inigoes, Maryland. (US Navy)

from conventional runways. Developed as part of a rapid deployment effort to fulfil an urgent operational need for a low-cost long-endurance unmanned ISR platform, the RQ-23A entered operational service in support of operations in Iraq and Afghanistan in 2006. Powered by a 32hp (23.5kW) Herbrandson two-stroke piston engine, the TigerShark has a maximum weight of 452lb (205kg) and an endurance of eight to ten hours. UX-24's RQ-23As serve as testbed platforms for a variety of payloads and other UAS systems.

First introduced in 2000, the RQ-26A Aerostar is powered by a 38hp (28kW) Zanzottera two-stroke boxer engine and weighs 530lb (240kg), with an endurance of 12 hours. Produced by Aeronautics Defense Systems in Israel, the Aerostar is classified as a Group 3 UAS. Utilised as a surrogate testbed for ISR equipment, the US Navy's Aerostar drones received the mission design series designation RQ-26A in 2014.

Although UX-24 had operated the MQ-8C variants of the Northrop Grumman Fire Scout vertical take-off and landing UAV (VTUAV), the squadron conducted its final flight in late 2024. Developed from the contractor's earlier MQ-8B, the Fire Scout utilised the airframe of the Bell model 407 light helicopter.

The Reaper is a Group 5 medium-altitude long-endurance (MALE) UAS that is operationally deployed by two US Marine Corps squadrons and a formal training unit. Produced by General Atomics, the MQ-9A replaced the Boeing Insitu RQ-21A previously operated by Marine Unmanned Aerial Vehicle Squadrons VMU-1 and VMU-3 and Marine Unmanned Aerial Vehicle Training Squadron VMUT-2. Developmental testing associated with the MQ-9A is carried out by UX-24 at Webster Field, which first received the Reaper in summer 2023. The unit is supporting efforts that are transforming the Reaper from a strike/ISR platform into an electronic warfare maritime domain awareness platform.

Avionics upgrades and payload integration testing will support the Reaper's initial operational capability in 2026. The Reaper will fill the USMC's requirement for a long-range, long-endurance, land-based UAS to conduct ISR and data relay in the Indo-Pacific. ■

The unmanned vehicle component of the US Navy's Blue Water logistics UAS takes off from the flight deck of Military Sealift Command's fleet replenishment oiler USNS 'Joshua Humphreys' (T-AO 188) while the ship was at sea in the Atlantic Ocean, on July 16, 2021. Operated by UX-24, the UAS flight proved the feasibility of using unmanned aircraft to transport small payloads of cargo from one ship to another while operating at sea. (US Navy/Bill Mesta)

A SkyTower II pod is positioned under the wing of an MQ-9A from UX-24 at Webster NOLF, Maryland, in preparation for a test mission. *(US Navy)*

An MQ-8C Fire Scout operated by UX-24 conducts a demonstration of the prototype single system multi-mission airborne mine detection (SMAMD) mine countermeasure at Eglin AFB, Florida, in May 2022. *(US Navy)*

Training the Testers

US Naval Test Pilot School (USNTPS)

Generally referred to as 'TPS', the US Naval Test Pilot School (USNTPS) is the Navy's primary source for flight test personnel. The school trains the world's finest developmental test pilots, naval flight officers, engineers, industry and international partners in full-spectrum test and evaluation of aircraft and aircraft systems. TPS is at the forefront in developing modern test techniques and is the only domestic source for rotary-wing test pilots, making it the dedicated test pilot school for the US Army.

The school has supported the development of US Naval Aviation for more than 80 years and provided the National Aeronautics and Space Administration (NASA) with nearly 100 astronauts including four of the original Mercury Seven. Its curriculum emphasises problem-solving under pressure, inter-service co-operation and a global perspective through partnerships with international test pilot schools and military air arms.

Located aboard Naval Air Station (NAS) Patuxent River, Maryland, the school is assigned as a component of the Naval Air Warfare Center Aircraft Division (NAWCAD) and reports to the Commander, Naval Test Wing Atlantic. TPS has been training test pilots since March 12, 1945, when the flight test pilots' training programme inducted its first class of 14 pilots and engineers. Created to formalise flight test instruction in response to high pilot fatality rates during World War Two, the part-time course included 37 hours of classroom instruction and just nine hours of flight time on aircraft borrowed from the NAS Patuxent River Flight Test Division.

A TA-4J Skyhawk that previously served the USNTPS is displayed at the school's entrance at NAS Patuxent River. (Tom Kaminski)

Aircraft types flown by the students were initially somewhat limited, but included the Grumman/General Motors FM-2 Wildcat and TBM Avenger, Grumman F6F Hellcat, Douglas SBD Dauntless and the North American SNJ Texan. Classes were held on Monday, Wednesday and Friday mornings and the course was spread over a ten-week period, with the first class (designated Class 0a) graduating on May 30, 1945. The curriculum included training in the fundamentals of aerodynamics, evaluation of aircraft stability and control characteristics, procedures for aircraft performance testing and flight test reporting, miscellaneous tests and trials and actual in-flight performance testing. A second class (designated Class 0b) was convened in October 1945 and graduated in February 1946.

In March 1946, the commander of the newly established Naval Air Test Center (NATC) at Patuxent 'Pax' River advised the US Chief of the Navy's Bureau of Aeronautics that a formal test pilot school should be established as a

Rockwell T-2C Buckeye trainers on the US Naval Test Pilot School ramp at NAS Patuxent River on July 6, 2004. Retirement of the Buckeyes followed the arrival of Beechcraft T-6s at the school. (Tom Kaminski)

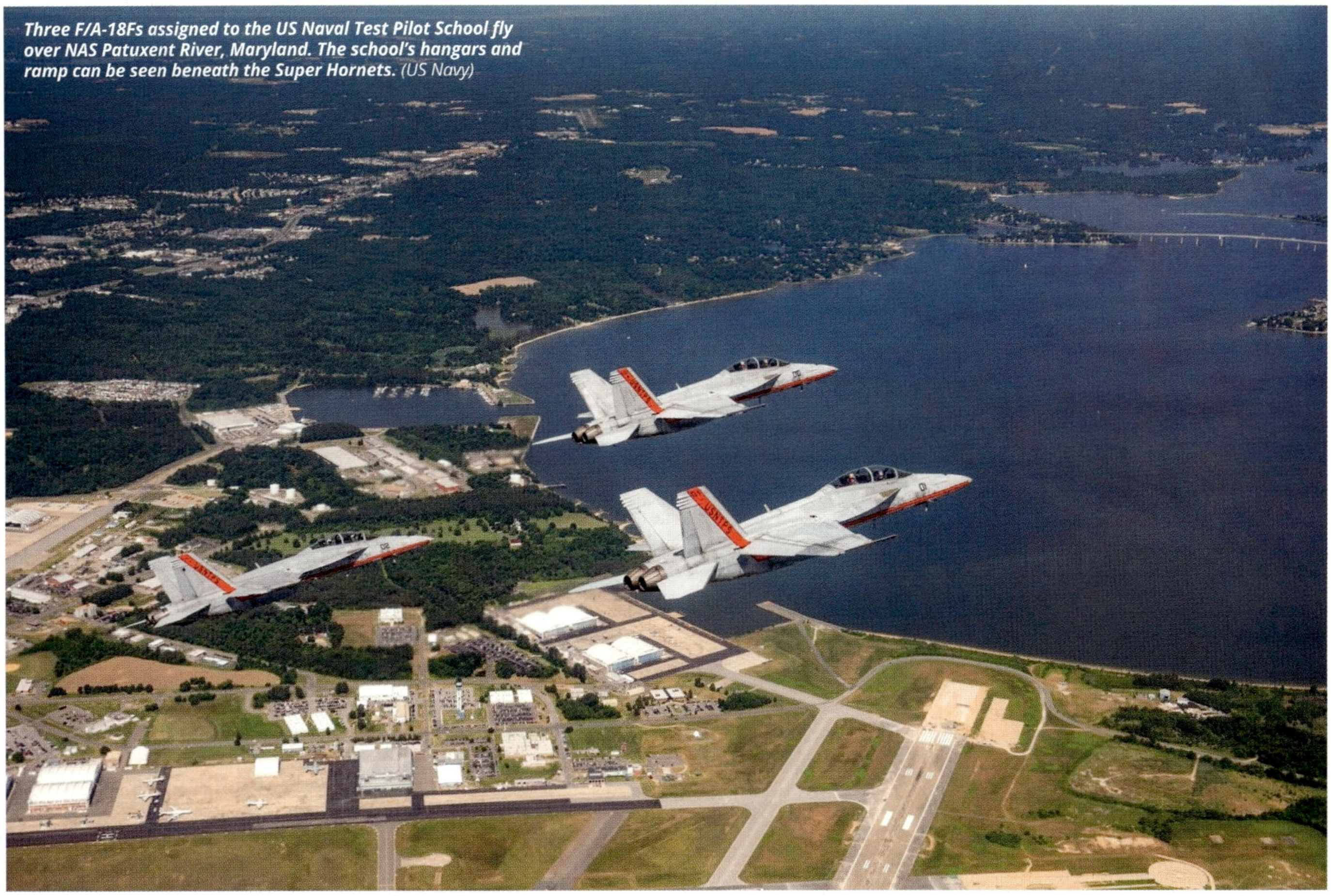
Three F/A-18Fs assigned to the US Naval Test Pilot School fly over NAS Patuxent River, Maryland. The school's hangars and ramp can be seen beneath the Super Hornets. (US Navy)

division of the test centre. He suggested that two classes of 30 students should be inducted annually and that the class length be expanded to four to five months. Although the bureau gave its approval for the school, post-war shortages of personnel and space caused the project to progress slowly.

In June 1946, Captain Frederick M Trapnell, for whom Pax River's airfield is named, became the NATC co-ordinator. Capt Trapnell had been a flight test officer with the Flight Test Group when it was located at NAS Anacostia in Washington DC, was the first US Navy pilot to fly a jet aircraft and was considered the best, most experienced naval test aviator of his generation.

He urged the Bureau of Aeronautics and the US Chief of Naval Operations to establish a full-time test pilot course. A formal plan, submitted in 1947, recommended inducting 30 new students every nine months at an estimated cost of $25,000 for the first year. On January 22, 1948, the Deputy Chief of Naval Operations authorised the establishment of the Test

"Over the course of the school's 80-year history, more than 4,800 students from 17 nations have graduated from its programmes"

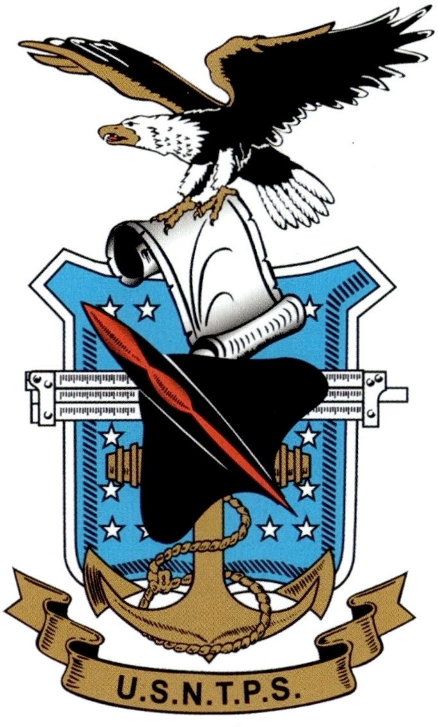

(US Naval Air Test Pilot School Insignia)

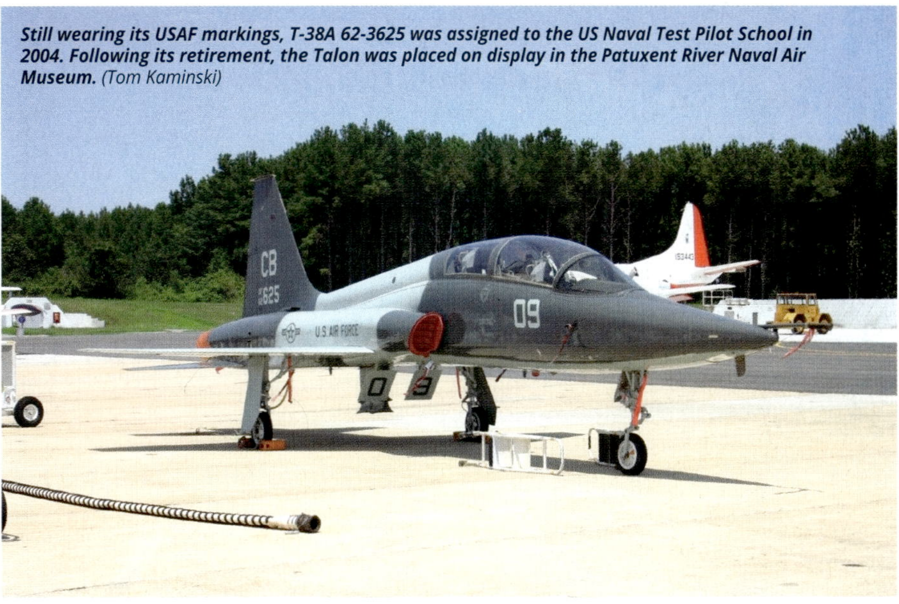

Still wearing its USAF markings, T-38A 62-3625 was assigned to the US Naval Test Pilot School in 2004. Following its retirement, the Talon was placed on display in the Patuxent River Naval Air Museum. (Tom Kaminski)

Pilot Training Division under the Naval Air Test Center.

The Test Pilot Training Division's Class 1 began on July 6, 1948, in borrowed facilities, with an assortment of used equipment. However, the newly established school had amassed some 550 technical books and acquired seven aircraft for training. The inventory initially included examples of the Beech SNB-1 Expediter, Consolidated PBY-6A Catalina and PB4Y-2 Privateer, Grumman F6F-5 Hellcat, F7F-3 Tigercat and F8F-1 Bearcat, and one of two prototype Fairchild XNQ-1 trainers. Although five classes had preceded them, on graduating on December 21, 1948, Class 1 became the Navy's first formal test pilots.

Over the years, the division continued to evolve and, in 1957, it was formally established taking on its current designation as the US Naval Test Pilot School. The course length was expanded to eight months in 1958 and a rotary-wing curriculum was added in 1961. Initially, each class included two helicopter pilots, but by 1975 ten were included in each new class. Naval flight officers (NFO) were added to the programme in 1966 and in 1973 the fixed and rotary-wing programmes were expanded to their current 11-month duration. The next major change came in 1975 when an 11-month airborne systems curriculum was added. TPS remains the only test pilot school that offers academic courses on helicopters for the US military. It is also the only test pilot school in the world with a dedicated airborne systems curriculum.

TPS is a squadron-level organisation within NAWC-AD and is led by Cmdr Travis Hartman, a 2009 graduate, who assumed command in June 2024. Besides occupying two hangars in building 110, the school finally gained a fixed home during June 1993, when a

A US Army UH-60L assigned to the US Naval Test Pilot School prepares to land at NAS Patuxent River on August 9, 2018. (US Navy)

purpose-built administrative and training facility opened in building 2168. In addition to classrooms and spaces for operations, mission planning and debrief, the facility contains a dedicated flying qualities simulator lab. It features programmable training devices that are capable of demonstrating a variety of fixed and rotary-wing aircraft configurations and another device that serves as a variable parameter radar trainer. The teaching staff includes military and civilian personnel comprising fixed-wing, rotary-wing and systems flight and academic instructors. Nearly 50 aircraft of 13 types assigned to the school are maintained by DynCorp, Airbus Helicopters and Precision Turbines under

contract to the Navy. DynCorp has provided logistics support and maintenance, including generating and recovering aircraft, for TPS since August 1973. The latter two contractors are responsible for maintaining the UH-72A helicopters and the C-26A ASTARS III for the school.

TPS Courses

The courses provided by TPS and its organisational structure have been revised continually so the school can accommodate new technology and more sophisticated aircraft. The curriculum is designed to prepare students to meet the demanding requirements of the US Navy and Army developmental test

The US Naval Test Pilot School's NU-1B Otter holds short of the runway while an F-35B prepares to land at NAS Patuxent River. The Otter is the last of its type in military service anywhere in the world. (US Navy)

and evaluation (DT&E) and operational test and evaluation (OT&E) organisations or the research, development, test and evaluation (RDT&E) activities within the other US or foreign military services. The fixed and rotary-wing programmes prepare pilots and engineers to evaluate aircraft performance and flying qualities and include instruction in airborne mission systems testing. The airborne systems programme is a comprehensive course covering airborne mission system test and evaluation for NFOs and engineers and includes instruction in aircraft performance and flying qualities. In addition to the normal 48-week programmes, in 1997 a Short Course Department was organised in 1997. The school offers several two-week short courses to personnel assigned to the Naval Air Warfare Center (NAWC), the Naval Air Systems Command (NAVAIR) and Army Aviation Technical Test Center (AATC):

- Introduction to Aircraft and Systems Test and Evaluation
- Introduction to Fixed-Wing Flying Qualities and Performance
- Introduction to Rotary-Wing Flying Qualities and Performance
- Introduction to Unmanned Aerial Systems Flight Test

One of five UH-72A helicopters operated by US Naval Test Pilot School departs St Mary's Regional Airport in Maryland during a training mission on October 17, 2020. (Mike Wilson)

Originally delivered to the US Air Force, C-26A 86-0456 taxies at NAS Patuxent River on June 29, 2018. The Metroliner was modified for the US Naval Test Pilot School and serves as an airborne systems training and research support (ASTARS) platform. (US Navy)

The US Naval Test Pilot School's 'flagship' T-38C 67-14856 carries a special paint scheme that features part of the school's insignia. (US Navy)

More recently, the school added an Advanced Flying Qualities Intermediate Course. The first group of civilian engineers from the inaugural class graduated on May 20, 2022. The eight-week course provides 140 hours of academic instruction, eight hours of simulator time and six flight events for each student. Special topics include reversible control systems, advanced flight control system evaluation, aircraft system identification methods and compressibility effects.

Two courses are convened by the TPS annually in January and July, and each comprises 36 students. Prior to starting the course, fixed-wing students will complete pre-arrival flight training in the T-6A at NAS Pensacola, Florida, and T-38C training at Joint Base San Antonio – Randolph, Texas. Likewise, rotary-wing students will receive training on the UH-72A and UH-60M at the Arizona Army National Guard's Western Army Aviation Training Site (WAATS) in Marana. In its early days, the majority of its students were flight test personnel assigned to the NATC, but today applications are accepted from throughout the fleet. Pilots and NFOs applying to the TPS must have a minimum of 1,000 hours of flight time and most have a background in engineering, mathematics or physics. However, on average, only ten per cent of those who apply are selected for admission. Besides US Navy and Marine Corps students, each class typically includes several US Army aviators and pilots from friendly foreign nations. In addition, the school maintains exchange programmes with the USAF Test Pilot School, France's Test Pilot School (EPNER) and the UK's Empire Test Pilot School (ETPS). Through these programmes, USAF and RAF pilots are typically assigned to each class. Less formal exchange agreements exist with France and Germany and personnel have made reciprocal visits at Russia's Gromov Flight Test Research Institute at Zhukovsky airfield near Moscow. Flight test engineers, who make up about 20 per cent of each class, come from both NAWCAD

One of five Lakota helicopters assigned to the US Naval Test Pilot School, UH-72A BuNo 168248 hover taxies at NAS Patuxent River on January 12, 2023. (US Navy)

One of three C-12Cs that support the US Naval Test Pilot School 78-23132 is owned by the US Army. The King Air is one of three types of Army aircraft used by the school. (Tom Kaminski)

and the NAWC Weapons Division at Naval Air Weapons Station (NAWS) China Lake and Naval Base Ventura County – Point Mugu, California. A typical class is best described using Class 166, which graduated on June 13, 2025, as an example. In addition to 19 US Navy and three USMC personnel, the graduates included five from the US Army and one the US Air Force, one US Coast Guard, civilian students and some personnel from the British Royal Air Force, Royal Australian and Royal Canadian Air Forces.

Over the course of the 48-week programme, students receive about 550 hours of academic instruction and fly around 100 sorties. Facilities, instructors and aircraft are shared by the two classes and while one class is flying the other is in class or writing reports. The students receive a great deal of instruction in varied subjects, including but not limited to aerodynamics, thermodynamics, flight systems, radar, electro-optical and navigation system theory, flight test preparation and conduct, data collection and reduction and test report preparation. Pilots and NFOs compile about 120 flight hours, and all students are required to prepare around 25 detailed reports describing the characteristics of a specific aircraft and/or aircraft system. On graduating from the 11-month programme, US Navy and US Marine Corps personnel are normally assigned to NAWCAD's test squadrons at NAS Patuxent River, NAWS China Lake, Naval Base Ventura County Point Mugu or Marine Corps Air Station (MCAS) Yuma, Arizona, for a 24 to 30-month tour. Army aviators who become experimental test pilots (XP) are normally assigned to the Redstone Test Center (RTC) at the Redstone Arsenal in Alabama or the Technology Development Directorate – Aviation (TDD-A) at Fort Eustis, Virginia.

Over the course of the programme, students rated on fixed-wing aircraft are exposed to rotary-wing types, often flying as co-pilots on the school's OH-58Cs. The reverse is true for the rotary-wing students who also get an opportunity to fly fixed-wing types. Army aviators entering the programme are dual-rated in fixed and rotary-wing types and fly both types. A variety of aircraft are assigned to the TPS and provide students with a broad spectrum of performance, flying qualities and weapon system capabilities.

Many of the aircraft are instrumented for data collection and equipped with a telemetry capability that allows data to be transmitted to ground stations. Besides regularly assigned assets, the TPS regularly borrows or bails aircraft from other military and civil sources that support the Qualitative Evaluation Program. These include warbirds, civil, experimental and other military aircraft. The TPS aircraft make around 4,700 flights totalling 6,700 flight hours annually.

Non-instructional duties are also assigned to TPS staff. These include investigating and

NP-3D BuNo 148889, on the ramp at NAS Patuxent River on July 5, 2004, served as an airborne systems training and research support (ASTARS) aircraft from 1975 to 2009. Although it was retired and subsequently scrapped, the Orion had served the US Naval Test Pilot School as a flying classroom. (Tom Kaminski)

Originally modified for electronic missions, EH-60A serial 87-24662 was reconfigured and assigned to the US Naval Test Pilot School as a training asset. It was later updated to UH-60L configuration. *(Tom Kaminski)*

developing advanced flight test techniques, conducting special projects and publishing manuals used by the aviation test community.

Training Fleet

The oldest aircraft in the TPS fleet include a de Havilland Canada NU-1B Otter and two U-6A Beavers. Powered by radial engines, ▶

AT-6E serial 20-1101 dips a wing on departure from Beech Field in Wichita, Kansas, on September 5, 2023. After a fuel stop in Kentucky, the Wolverine flew to NAS Patuxent River in Maryland, where it was handed over to the US Naval Test Pilot School. *(Textron Aviation/Tyler Mabie)*

USNTPS Aircraft Inventory – October 2025		
Airbus Helicopters	UH-72A Lakota	(5)
Beech Aircraft	C-12C Huron	(3)
Beech Aircraft	T-6B Texan II	(6)
Beech Aircraft	AT-6E Wolverine	(2)
Bell Helicopter	OH-58C Kiowa	(4)
Boeing	F/A-18F Super Hornet	(3)
de Havilland Canada	NU-1B Otter	(1)
de Havilland Canada	U-6A Beaver	(2)
Fairchild Aircraft	C-26A Metro III	(1)
Learjet	Lear 25*	(1)
Northrop Grumman	T-38C Talon	(10)
Schweizer Aircraft	X-26A Frigate	(2)
Sikorsky Aircraft	UH-60L* Blackhawk	(5)

* Owned by Calspan Aerospace

UH-72A BuNo 168246 awaits its clearance for take-off while one of the US Naval Test Pilot School's U-6As makes its final approach to land at NAS Patuxent River. The school's five Lakotas replaced Hughes OH-6Bs that were originally delivered to the US Army. (US Navy)

the 'bush planes' give students unique experience with earlier, less sophisticated designs. Based on the de Havilland Canada DHC-3, a single NU-1B Otter has been part of the TPS curriculum since October 1966. It is the oldest aircraft on the US Navy inventory and is reportedly the last Otter in military service worldwide. It was originally used in support of scientific research missions to the Antarctic when it was delivered to the Navy. The Otter is used to demonstrate low-speed aircraft handling, fixed-wing short take-off and landing (STOL) qualities, flight characteristics and directional stability techniques. As a 'taildragger', the aircraft's unique high wing and tail wheel configuration provides a different flight experience from more common tricycle landing gear-equipped aircraft. Delivered to the Navy in September 1956, the Otter was originally assigned the designation UC-1A.

Although smaller than the NU-1B, the school's U-6As duplicate the roles of the Otter. Additionally, the Beavers are used as tow airplanes for the school's X-26A gliders. The U-6A is based on the de Havilland Canada DHC-2 airframe. Both the school's U-6As were originally delivered to the US Army and USAF and assigned the designation L-20A.

The TPS uses a pair of Schweizer X-26A Frigate gliders for flying qualities and to increase the student's knowledge of the dynamics of flight. The Frigates are used to demonstrate the characteristics of unpowered

Three F/A-18Fs assigned to the US Naval Test Pilot School fly over Chesapeake Bay near NAS Patuxent River, Maryland. The Super Hornets regularly support the school's airborne systems programme. (US Navy)

One of several aircraft modified by Calspan as variable stability training platforms, Lear 24D N101VS was often used by the US Naval Test Pilot School until its retirement in October 2017. In addition to training duties, the aircraft support flight tests when required. (Calspan)

aircraft, including the energy management and the unique yaw/roll characteristics associated with high aspect ratio wings. They also support high lift to drag evaluations, un-powered flying qualities training and aerobatics. Based on the Schweizer SGS 2-32 sailplane, the first of the two-seat, high-performance gliders entered service with the school in August 1968.

The US Naval Test Pilot School at NAS Pax River acquired five T-38As in 1969, and it currently operates ten Talons that have been upgraded to T-38C configuration. The upgrade that brought the Talons to the T-38C configuration was completed in December 2016. The supersonic Talons fly around 1,100 hours each year, providing students with experience evaluating its performance, flying qualities, dynamics, and transonic and supersonic flight characteristics and to teach aircraft handling and flight characteristics, transonic performance and system integration.

The school has operated the Beechcraft T-6B since 2010, when the first advanced primary trainers arrived to replace earlier T-6A variants that entered service in September 2005. The Texan IIs support basic pilot skills training, teach fundamental flight test and evaluation techniques, provide a digital avionics experience and serve as a foundation for follow-on training, fundamental flight test and evaluation techniques.

Owned by the US Army, three Beech Aircraft C-12Cs support multi-engine familiarisation, asymmetric power effects and navigation systems evaluations as well as handling qualities and performance instructions. The King Airs replaced older Beech Aircraft U-21Fs in 1999. Despite their age, the aircraft have been updated with digital 'glass' instrumentation.

The USNTPS took delivery of its first F/A-18F Super Hornet in July 2010 and to replace older F/A-18D Hornets used by the school. The aircraft are some of the oldest Super Hornets in service and were produced as part of the first low rate initial production batch. Although each student receives at least one flight in the school's F/A-18Fs, the Super Hornets primarily support the aircraft systems curriculum.

The school's most recent acquisition comprised a pair of Beechcraft AT-6E Wolverines that were transferred from the USAF when they were no longer required by the service. The light attack aircraft were delivered in September 2023 and have augmented TPS's fixed-wing and systems syllabus.

Rotary-wing instruction platforms include the Airbus Helicopters UH-72A Lakota, Bell OH-58C Kiowa and Sikorsky UH-60L Blackhawk. As part of the core test pilot curriculum the school's five fully instrumented UH-72As support flying qualities and performance, integrated systems training and AFCS evaluations. The Lakotas replaced the school's Hughes TH-6Bs, beginning in November 2009 when the initial pair arrived.

Five US Army-owned UH-60Ls support flying qualities and performance training. The first UH-60Ls arrived to replace the earlier UH-60As in 2015. One of the Black Hawks was modified with a new variable stability system (VSS) in 2015 and is capable of simulating a large variety of handling characteristics. Four Army-owned OH-58Cs are the last examples of the Kiowa in US service. The light observation helicopters support flying qualities and performance training and are used for autorotational landing evaluations.

The school also operates a Fairchild C-26A Metroliner as an airborne systems training and research support (ASTARS). The ASTARS III is equipped with a Leonardo Vixen 500E active electronically scanned array (AESA) radar, Wescam MX-15 HD electro-optical/infrared sensor turret, video recording systems and operator consoles. Elbit Systems of America's M7 Aerospace subsidiary developed the ASTARS III under a $7.5m contract awarded by US Naval Air Systems Command (NAVAIR) in May 2016. The Navy-owned C-26A replaced a Calspan Saab SF340 that had been used in the role as ASTARS II under contract. ■

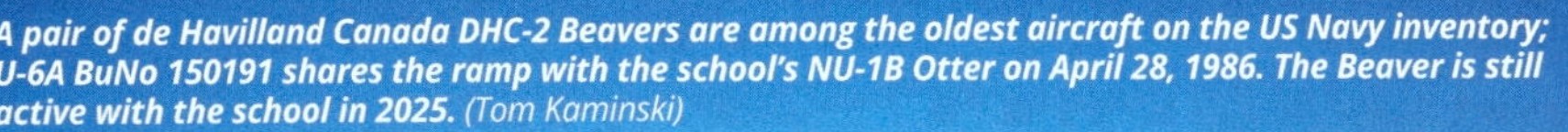

A pair of de Havilland Canada DHC-2 Beavers are among the oldest aircraft on the US Navy inventory; U-6A BuNo 150191 shares the ramp with the school's NU-1B Otter on April 28, 1986. The Beaver is still active with the school in 2025. (Tom Kaminski)

Supporting the Fleet

Commander, US Fleet Readiness Centers

O ften overlooked, the US Navy's intermediate and depot-level maintenance organisations serve a very important role in keeping the fleet ready to carry out its missions. Following the recommendations made by the 2005 Base Realignments and Closures (BRAC) commission, the Navy reorganised its aviation maintenance units and established several Fleet Readiness Centers (FRC) under the Naval Air Systems Command (NAVAIR). Designed to support the Naval Aviation Enterprise's (NAE), plans for transforming naval aviation maintenance, the FRCs replaced the

The first US Navy CMV-22B inducted for maintenance at FRCE awaits attention at MCAS Cherry Point, North Carolina, on September 5, 2024. The depot services all three variants of the Osprey tiltrotor, which include the Marine Corps MV-22B and the USAF CV-22B. (US Navy)

FA-18C BuNo 164645 from strike fighter squadron VFA-25 undergoes depot-level maintenance with Fleet Readiness Center Southwest at NAS North Island in Coronado, California, on June 16, 2005. *(Tom Kaminski)*

A weight and handling technician helps to stabilise an F/A-18 fuselage as it is repositioned using a crane as part of a centre barrel replacement (CBR) maintenance evolution at Fleet Readiness Center Southeast (FRCSE) on August 4, 2023. CBRs were conducted to extend the service life of F-18A-D series aircraft.
(US Navy/Toiete Jackson)

(Fleet Readiness Center Insignia)

Aircraft Intermediate Maintenance Departments (AIMD) and Naval Aviation Depots (NADEP) that had previously carried out intermediate and depot-level maintenance for the fleet. The transformation began when the Commander, Fleet Readiness Command (COMFRC) was established at Naval Air Station (NAS) Patuxent River, Mayland, along with six FRCs on October 10, 2006. Rear Admiral Anthony E 'Tony' Rossi has served as COMFRC since July 2025. ➤

Commander, Fleet Readiness Centers (COMFRC) – NAS Patuxent River, Maryland	
FRC Mid-Atlantic	NAS Oceana, Virginia
FRC Mid-Atlantic Detachment Norfolk	Chambers Field, NS Norfolk, Virginia
FRC Mid-Atlantic Det Patuxent River	NAS Patuxent River, Maryland
FRC Mid-Atlantic Det Oceana	NAS Oceana, Virginia
FRC Mid-Atlantic Det Voyage Repair Team	Naval Station Norfolk, Virginia
FRC East	MCAS Cherry Point, N.C.
FRC East Det Beaufort	MCAS Beaufort, South Carolina
FRC East Det Hurlburt Field	Hurlburt Field, Florida
FRC East Det Kinston	North Carolina Global TransPark, Kinston Regional Jetport, North Carolina
FRC East Det New River	MCAS New River, North Carolina
FRC Southeast	NAS Jacksonville, Florida
FRC Southeast Det Jacksonville	NAS Jacksonville, Florida
FRC Southeast Det Mayport	NS Mayport, Florida
FRC Southeast Det Key West	NAS Key West, Florida
FRC Southeast Det Cecil Field	Cecil Airport, Jacksonville, Florida
FRC Southeast Det Tinker AFB	Tinker AFB, Oklahoma
FRC Northwest	NAS Whidbey Island, Washington
FRC Northwest Det Everett	Naval Station Everett, Washington
FRC West	NAS Lemoore, California
FRC West Det Lemoore	NAS Lemoore, California
FRC West Det Fallon	NAS Fallon, Nevada
FRC West Det China Lake	NAWS China Lake, California
FRC Southwest	NAS North Island, California
FRC Southwest Det North Island	NAS North Island, California
FRC Southwest Det Point Mugu	NB Ventura County-Point Mugu, California
FRC Southwest Site Miramar	MCAS Miramar, California
FRC Southwest Site Camp Pendleton	MCAS Camp Pendleton, California
FRC Southwest Site Yuma	MCAS Yuma, Arizona
FRC Southwest Det Kaneohe Bay	MCAS Kaneohe Bay, Hawaii
FRC Southwest Det Cannon AFB	Cannon AFB, New Mexico
FRC Western Pacific	NAF Atsugi, Japan
FRC Western Pacific Det Iwakuni, Japan	MCAS Iwakuni, Japan
FRC Western Pacific Det Okinawa	MCAS Futenma, Japan
FRC Western Pacific Det. Guam	Andersen AFB, Guam
FRC Western Pacific Det CENTCOM	Andersen AFB, Guam
FRC Reserve Mid-West	NAS JRB Fort Worth, Texas
FRC Reserve Mid-West Det McGuire	Joint Base McGuire-Dix-Lakehurst, New Jersey
FRC Reserve Mid-West Det New Orleans	NAS JRB New Orleans, Louisiana
FRC Reserve Mid-West Det Washington	JB Andrews-NAF Washington, Maryland
FRC Reserve Mid-West Det Fort Worth	NAS JRB Fort Worth, Texas

The FRCs trace their history to the establishment of the NAS San Diego Assembly and Repair Department in 1919. Similar departments were respectively established at NAS Jacksonville in Florida and Marine Corps Air Station (MCAS) Cherry Point, North Carolina, in 1940 and December 1943.

The departments were later renamed as Overhaul and Repair Departments before becoming Naval Air Rework Facilities (NARF) in April 1967 and Naval Aviation Depots (NADEP) in April 2001.

Today, COMFRC oversees three depots, ten intermediate-level and 25 tenant sites, located in five countries and territories, and 13 states. It has a skilled workforce of approximately 12,000 civilians, 6,000 sailors and marines and 3,000 contractors. As part of the Naval Aviation Fleet Infrastructure Optimization Plan (FIOP) the FRCs are being modernised to provide increased capability and capacity across the Naval Aviation Enterprise. Begun in 2021, the FIOP is a ten-year programme that transforms aviation depots into modernised maintenance, repair and overhaul (MRO) repair centres. As a result, the FRCs will be better positioned to maintain aircraft, powerplants, components and support equipment.

Currently, three of the of nine FRCs – FRC East, FRC Southeast and FRC Southwest – are considered full MRO complexes and perform depot-level maintenance and modifications of aircraft, engines, weapons, components and equipment. The remaining locations are more limited, conducting intermediate-level maintenance and repair support. Three major FRC shore-based intermediate-level facilities comprise FRC Mid-Atlantic, FRC West and FRC Northwest. They provide unscheduled repair and some limited depot-level aircraft MRO at the fleet's three master jet bases – NAS Oceana in Virginia, NAS Lemoore in California and NAS Whidbey Island, Washington.

- FRC Mid-Atlantic
- FRC East
- FRC Southeast
- FRC Northwest
- FRC West
- FRC Southwest
- FRC Western Pacific
- FRC Reserve
- FRC Reserve Mid-West

Fleet Readiness Center Mid-Atlantic (FRCMA)

Headquartered at NAS Oceana in Virginia Beach, FRCMA was established on October

Personnel from FRCSE tow an F-35B from Marine Fighter Attack Squadron VMFA-122 at NAS Jacksonville, Florida, on August 8, 2024. The Lightning II was the first F-35 inducted into the depot and was part of a readiness improvement initiative to support corrosion mitigation efforts. *(US Navy/Toiete Jackson)*

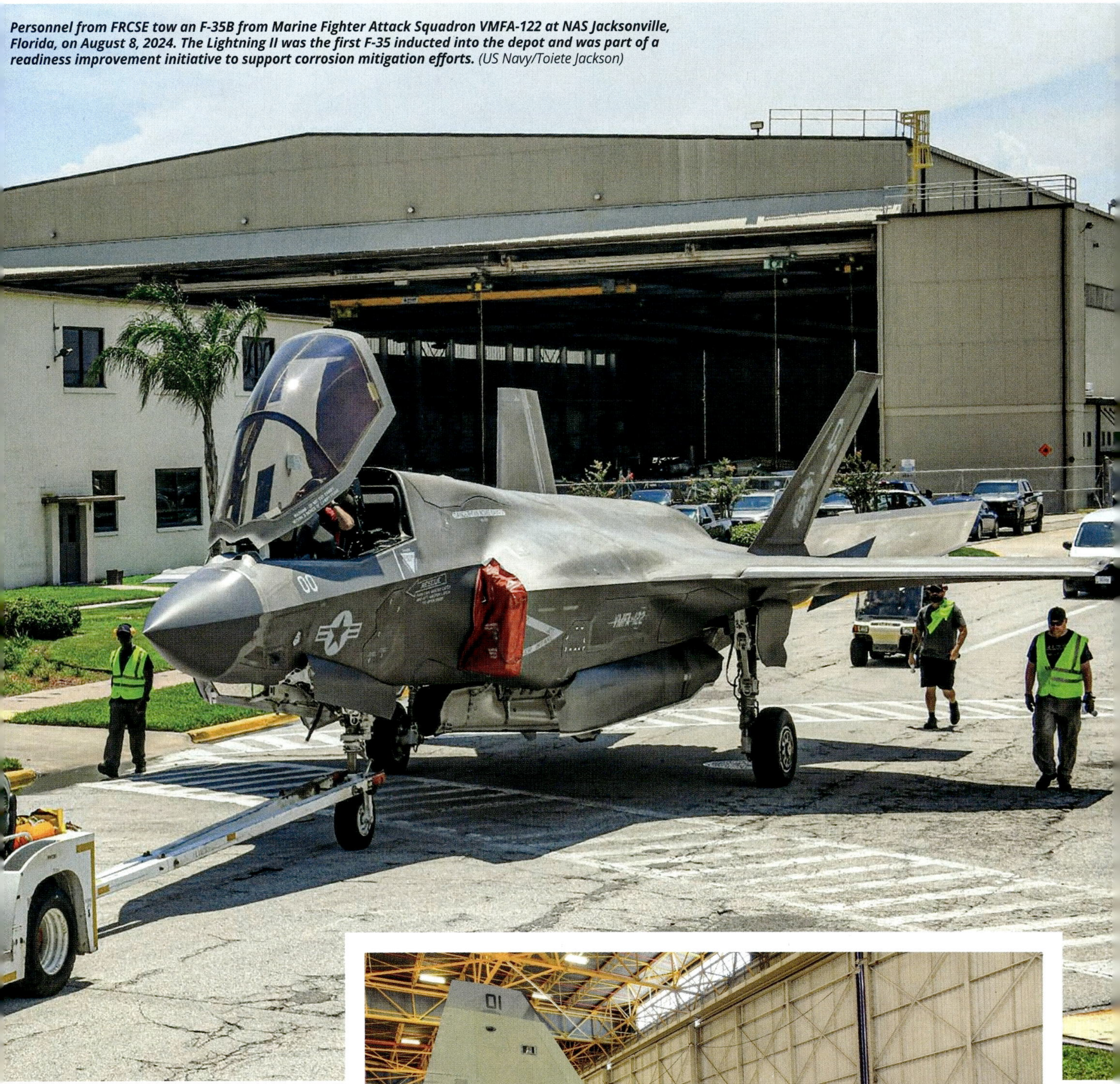

27, 2008, when Commander, Strike Fighter Wing Atlantic Detachment Aircraft Intermediate Maintenance Department (AIMD) Oceana was redesignated. It performs scheduled maintenance inspection and repair, unscheduled emergency in-service repair, structural and electronic system modifications on numerous carrier-based aircraft. FRCMA covers different sites: FRCMA Detachments Oceana, Norfolk and Patuxent River, Voyage Repair Team (VRT) Norfolk and Mayport, and FRCMA Aircraft Department Oceana and Norfolk. The organisation was originally established as Commander, Fighter Wing Atlantic Det AIMD Oceana, on March 14, 2002. The VRT performs depot-level maintenance and repairs on aircraft launch and recovery equipment (ALRE) that includes jet

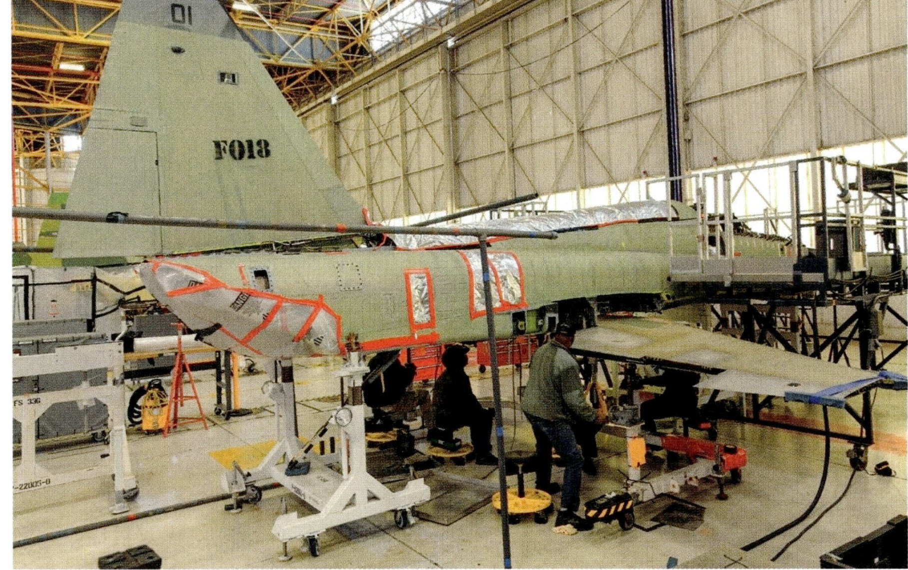

Technicians assigned to Fleet Readiness Center Southeast's F-5 production line prepare to remove the wing of an F-5N Tiger II for inspection at NAS Jacksonville, Florida, on February 13, 2023. *(US Navy/Toiete Jackson)*

The last Legacy Hornet to receive depot maintenance with the FRCSW at NAS North Island was returned to service in October 2024. (US Navy)

blast deflectors, catapult systems and arresting systems.

Fleet Readiness Center East (FRCE)

Located at MCAS Cherry Point in Havelock, North Carolina, the centre was named the MCAS Cherry Point Overhaul and Repair (O&R) Department when it was opened December 16, 1943. In April 1967, it became known as the Naval Air Rework Facility Cherry Point. In March 1987, the facility was renamed Naval Aviation Depot (NADEP) Cherry Point, then Naval Air Depot Cherry Point in April 2001. Following the recommendations of the 2005 Base Realignment and Closure (BRAC) Commission, the facility was realigned and its name changed to Fleet Readiness Center East on March 14, 2008. FRCE occupies 119 structures

on 147 acres, covering a total of 2.1 million sq ft at MCAS Cherry Point. The MV-22B, CMV-22B and CV-22B, AH-1Z, UH-1Y, CH-53E/K, MH-53E, F-35A/B/C and the C-130T, KC-130J/T are all maintained by the FRCE.

North Carolina Global TransPark, Kinston Regional Jetport is home to FRC East Detachment Kinston. The satellite facility overhauls and maintains USAF UH-1N Twin Huey helicopters. Opened in March 2021, the facility is undergoing expansion that began in June 2024. When completed by September 2026, the 700,000sq ft MRO complex will maintain and repair C-130T, KC-130J/T aircraft and the USAF's HH 60W and MH-139A helicopters.

The FRCE marked the end of an era when it completed the final AV-8B maintenance event and delivered the Harrier II to Marine

Attack Squadron VMA-223 at Cherry Point on September 26, 2024. The first CMV-22B was inducted for maintenance on August 21, 2024.

FRCE detachments at MCAS New River in North Carolina and MCAS Beaufort, South Carolina, support the based MV-22B, AH-1Z and UH-1Y helicopters and the F/A-18C/D. Another detachment located at the USAF's Hurlburt Field in Florida supports the CV-22B Osprey.

Fleet Readiness Center Southeast (FRCSE)

As *the largest tenant command* at NAS Jacksonville, the FRC is also the largest industrial employer in northeast Florida and southeast Georgia. The depot, which consists of 70 buildings that cover 127 acres, was originally founded as Naval Air Rework Facility

FRCE at MCAS Cherry Point marked the end of an era when it completed delivery of its final AV-8B maintenance event. The Harrier II was delivered to Marine Attack Squadron VMA-223 at Cherry Point on September 26, 2024. (US Navy)

An MH-60S was one of eight Seahawks undergoing scheduled depot-level maintenance at NIPPI Corporation's facility near Naval Air Facility Atsugi, Japan, in mid-2021. The company carries out depot-level maintenance under contract from FRC WESTPAC. *(US Navy)*

(NARF) Jacksonville and established in 1940. It was redesignated as Naval Aviation Depot Jacksonville in March 1987, then Naval Air Depot Jacksonville, in April 2001. The facility assumed its current identity on March 14, 2008. Additionally, FRC Southeast maintains intermediate-level detachments at Naval Air Station Jacksonville, Naval Station Mayport and Naval Air Station Key West in Florida.

FRCSE is responsible for work associated with the F/A-18 Hornet/Super Hornet, F-5 Tiger II, T-6 A/B Texan, T-44 Pegasus, MH-60 Seahawk, HH-60 Pave Hawk, P-8 Poseidon and E-6 Mercury aircraft. FRCSE inducted its first F-35B Lightning II and F135 power module (PM), in August 2024. The first CMV-22B was inducted on August 21, 2024. Work on the first USAF T-6A was completed in January 2021. A satellite MRO facility at Cecil Airport in Jacksonville is operated by Boeing and supports the F/A-18C/D/E/F.

FRCSE added a new capability when the first two T-45C trainers were inducted into the Service Life Extension Program (SLEP) production line. The aircraft arrived at the facility in July 2025, just 13 months after the US Navy identified the requirement. Whereas one of the Goshawks will undergo a wing swap, the second will receive the full scope of SLEP work. Under the wing swap programme, the trainers exchange their wings with sets that have already been repaired, enabling more efficient turnaround times. The work is supported by V2X, which currently manages all T-45 organisational-level, intermediate-level and depot-level maintenance for the Navy. The FRCSE expects to conduct the T-45 repairs through 2036.

Fleet Readiness Center Northwest (FRCNW)

The tenant activity at NAS Whidbey Island, in Oak Harbor, Washington, was originally activated in 1959 as the Aircraft Intermediate Maintenance Detachment. It was later formally established as the Commander, VAQ Wing Pacific Detachment AIMD in January 2001 and assumed its current designation on October 20, 2008. It primarily supports Whibey Island's based EA-168G electronic combat jets and Boeing P-8A multi-mission aircraft.

Fleet Readiness Center West (FRCW)

Established on November 4, 2008, at NAS Lemoore in California's Central Valley, the air station is situated between Los Angeles and San Francisco around 40 miles south of Fresno. It is the Navy's largest master jet base. FRCW supports and maintains Lemoore's large Super Hornet and growing Lightning II fleets. When it was created, FRCW combined Aircraft Intermediate Maintenance Department (AIMD) Lemoore with Naval Aviation Depot (NADEP) North Island Det Lemoore. Detachments were established at NAS Fallon in Nevada, by combining AIMD Fallon and NADEP North Island Det Fallon, and FRCW Det China Lake was formed from AIMD China Lake at Naval Air Weapons Station China Lake, California.

Fleet Readiness Center Southwest (FRCSW)

Located at NAS North Island in Coronado, California, FRCSW's history can be traced to 1919 when the US Department of War established its first aviation maintenance and repair facility. The largest of the Navy's FRCs is considered to be the birthplace of US Naval Aviation maintenance. FRCSW encompasses sites at NAS North Island, MCAS Miramar and MCAS Camp Pendleton and NAS Lemoore in California, MCAS Yuma in Arizona, Cannon AFB in New Mexico and MCAS Kaneohe Bay in Hawaii and detachments at Naval Base Ventura County-Point Mugu in California and NAS Fallon, Nevada.

The FRCSW is the MRO centre for the E-2C/D, C-2A, F/A-18E/F, EA-18G, MV/CMV/CV-22B, AH-1Z, UH-1Y, CH-53E, MH-60R/S and MQ-4C. It completed overhaul work on the final Legacy ▶

A USAF UH-1N undergoes ground checks in preparation for its first flight after maintenance at FRCE. The depot repairs and services Twin Huey helicopters at a dedicated facility in Kinston's North Carolina Global TransPark. *(US Navy)*

An F-35B assigned to Marine Fighter Attack Squadron VMFA-122 prepares to park after landing at NAS Jacksonville in Florida on August 7, 2024. The Lightning II was the first to be inducted into the FRCSE depot for maintenance. *(US Navy/Toiete Jackson)*

An MV-22B is temporarily parked on the flight line at Naval Air Facility Atsugi in Japan following its arrival. The Osprey was subsequently moved to the NIPPI Corporation's aviation maintenance facility for scheduled depot-level maintenance. (FRC WESTPAC)

An overhauled CH-53E departs FRCE during a post maintenance flight at MCAS Cherry Point. (Fleet Readiness Center East/Joe Andes)

FRCE at MCAS Cherry Point inducted the depot's first CH-53K on April 4, 2024. The King Stallion arrived from Marine Heavy Helicopter Squadron HMH-461 and is the first of four CH-53Ks that will undergo routine maintenance at FRCE as part of the Age Exploration Program Depot (AEPD) project. (US Navy)

Hornet when F/A-18D was returned to the fleet in October 2024.

The centre inducted the first F/A-18F to undergo the service life modification (SLM) at a naval aviation depot in June 2022. In addition to extending the operational life of the F/A-18E/F from 6,000 to 7,500 hours, the programme incorporates Block III capabilities. The first SLM Super Hornet was completed at the Boeing facility in St Louis, Missouri, in 2018 and the company's facility in San Antonio, Texas, completed its first SLM in January 2021

Responsibility for the F-16C/D arrived in late 2023 when the first adversary aircraft was inducted for programmed structural sustainment and repair (PSSR).

During 2024, the FRCSW completed work on 144 aircraft against a target of 140. Highlights included completion of the last Legacy F/A-18 centre barrel aircraft (RA52) and completing eight Super Hornet SLMs.

Fleet Readiness Center Western Pacific (FRC WESTPAC)

Headquartered at Naval Air Facility Atsugi, Japan, FRC WESTPAC provides intermediate and depot-level repairs to forward-deployed aviation units. It had detachments at NAF Atsugi, MCASs Iwakuni and Futenma Okinawa in Japan, Busan in Korea and Naval Support Activity Bahrain in Manama. The organisation first stood up in the mid-1950s and was known as the Fleet Air Western Pacific Rework Activity (FAWPRA). On October 1, 1980, FAWPRA was renamed the Naval Air Pacific Repair Activity (NAPRA) and assumed its current designation on October 1, 2008.

FRC WESTPAC supports more than two dozen different models of aircraft and provides in-service repairs (ISRs), support of shipboard aircraft launch and recovery

An F-5N is prepared for post-maintenance functional check flight carried out by the FRCSE Adversary Aircraft Production team on March 1, 2021. An FCF tests the aircraft and all its systems to ensure they work properly. (US Navy/Toiete Jackson)

equipment and engineering and logistics support to NAVAIR and programme executive offices (PEO) via Fleet Support Teams (FST).

To supplement the fleet's own organic workforce, FRC Westpac contracts out some of its maintenance and repair work to commercial aviation MRO facilities in the region. In addition to providing a more agile response to aviation maintenance the contractors deliver savings by eliminating costly aircraft relocation and down time.

Fleet Readiness Center Reserve Mid-West (FRCRMW)

The Reserve Aviation Maintenance Center of Excellence is headquartered at NAS Joint Reserve Base (JRB) Fort Worth in Texas. FRCRMW is responsible for four detachments located at facilities that primarily support US Navy and Marine Corps Reserve aviation units. They comprise Detachment McGuire at Joint Base McGuire-Dix-Lakehurst in New Jersey, Detachment New Orleans at NAS JRB New Orleans in Louisiana, Detachment Washington at JB Andrews-Naval Air Facility Washington in Maryland and Detachment Fort Worth at NAS JRB Fort Worth, Texas. Each is tasked with providing intermediate-level maintenance in support of the units assigned to the respective bases.

In addition to FRC's own facility the command receives maintenance support from several domestic and international MRO contractors, including:

- AAR Corporation, Oklahoma City, Oklahoma
- L3Harris Technologies, Waco, Texas
- Northrop Grumman, Lake Charles, Louisiana
- Cascade Aerospace, Abbotsford British Columbia, Canada
- Korean Air Aerospace Division, Busan, Republic of Korea
- Marshall Aerospace and Defence Group, Cambridge, England
- NIPPI Corporation, Yamato, Japan
- Subaru Corporation, Kisarazu, Japan ∎

Personnel assigned to the FRCE F-35 Lightning II aircraft modification line confer with a pilot prior to the start of a functional check flight inspection for an F-35B at MCAS Cherry Point. The aircraft was the 150th Lightning II inducted by the depot. FRCE is the lead site for depot-level maintenance on the F-35B and has conducted modifications and repair on the aircraft since 2013. FRCE also works with the F-35A and F-35C Lightning II variants. (Fleet Readiness Center East/Joe Andes)

FRCSE personnel lower the fuselage of a T-6 trainer onto its wing assembly. The facility was awarded the maintenance contract for Texan II repairs in November 2017. (US Navy/Victor Pitts)

A mixed formation of VX-30 'Bloodhounds' and VX-31 'Dust Devils' aircraft – including the P-3C Orion, Gulfstream NC-37B, E-2D Advanced Hawkeye, KC-130T Hercules, F/A-18E Super Hornet, AV-8B+ Harrier and EA-18G Growler – flies over San Nicolas Island and Point Mugu's Sea Range during a photo exercise on January 8, 2025. *(US Navy/Katie Archibald)*

West Coast Weapons Testing

Naval Air Warfare Center Weapons Division

(Naval Air Warfare Center Weapons Division Insignia)

Assigned to the Pacific Missile Test Center, a Grumman A-6E Intruder receives maintenance between flights at NAS Point Mugu, California, on October 11, 1990. (Mike Anselmo)

The Naval Air Warfare Center Weapons Division (NAWCWD) is the Naval Air Systems Command's organisation dedicated to maintaining a centre of excellence in weapons development for the US Department of the Navy. Headquartered at Naval Air Weapons Station (NAWS) China Lake, California, NAWCWD primarily conducts operations from two locations in Southern California. The command operates a number of laboratories and facilities that conduct weapons research, development, acquisition, test and evaluation from NAWS China Lake and Naval Base Ventura County – Point Mugu (NBVC).

Established on January 21, 1992, the NAWCWD combined operations at four Navy shore facilities that comprised the Naval Weapons Evaluation Facility (NWEF) at Kirtland AFB in New Mexico, the Naval Ordnance Missile Test Station at White Sands in New Mexico, the Pacific Missile Test Center (PMTC) at NAWS Point Mugu, California, and the Naval Weapons Center (NWC) at NAWS China Lake, California. NAWCAD serves as the US Navy's "full-spectrum research, development, test and evaluation (RDT&E) engineering support

>

A BQM-34 unmanned aerial vehicle launches from Point Mugu during a test of the US Navy's solid fuel integral rocket ramjet (SFIRR) demonstrator, developed by Naval Air Warfare Center Weapons Division. The test marked the first air launch of SFIRR from an unmanned platform. *(US Navy)*

FA-18D BuNo 165860 from Air Test and Evaluation Squadron VX-31 operates over the California's Sierra Nevada mountains during a test mission in July 2023. *(US Navy)*

and fleet-support centre for air platforms, autonomous air vehicles, missiles and missile subsystems, weapon systems associated with air warfare and sensor systems used to conduct anti-submarine warfare from air platforms".

It is the Navy's premier test, training and experimentation centre for weapons systems associated with air warfare, missiles and missile subsystems, aircraft weapons integration and airborne electronic warfare systems.

Point Mugu

Originally established on November 29, 1945, as part of the stand-up of the NAWCWD, NAS Point Mugu was redesignated NAWS Point Mugu on January 21, 1992. The facility reverted to Naval Air Station status on December 2, 1998, but was consolidated with Naval Construction Battalion Center (NCBC) Port Hueneme to form Naval Base Ventura County on October 6, 2000.

NBVC's coastal location in Oxnard is around 30 miles north of Los Angeles and NAWCWD Point Mugu is its largest tenant. It is responsible for management of the Point Mugu Sea Range (PMSR) and serves as the Navy's centre of electronic warfare expertise. NAWCWD provides logistics and in-service support for guided missiles, free-fall weapons, targets, support equipment, crew systems and electronic warfare. In recent years, the Point Mugu facility has supported the RDT&E and fielding of several unmanned air systems including the Northrop Grumman MQ-8B and MQ-8C Fire Scout vertical tactical unmanned air vehicle (VTUAV) and the high-altitude, long-endurance (HALE) MQ-4C Triton.

Test operations at Point Mugu are conducted by air test and evaluation squadron VX-30. The Point Mugu facility consists of 4,500 acres and includes facilities on the nearby Laguna Peak. It provides an elevated line-of-sight

An F/A-18F and EA-18Gs from Air Test and Evaluation Squadrons VX-9 and VX-31 line the ramp at Naval Base Ventura County, Point Mugu, California, during the Gray Flag 2024 exercise on September 18, 2024. *(US Navy/Katie Archibald)*

A VX-31 'Dust Devils' AV-8B+ flies over Point Mugu's Sea Range during a photo exercise on January 6, 2025. The squadron flew its final Harrier II flight on September 23, 2025. (US Navy/Katie Archibald)

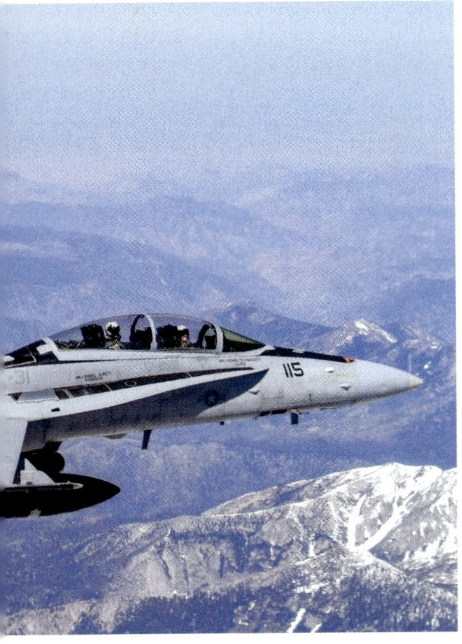

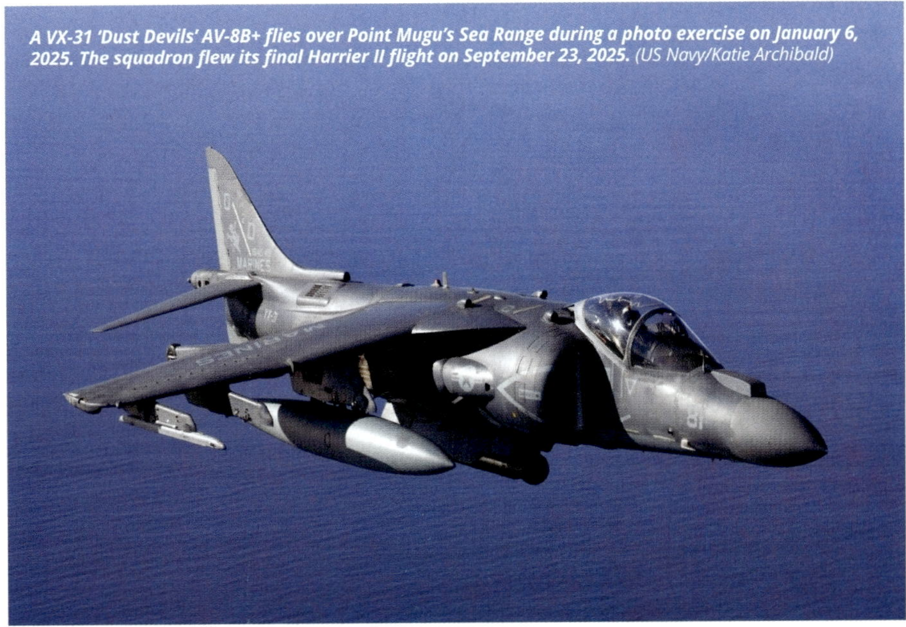

for extended instrumentation coverage of the PMSR, including line-of-sight surface surveillance radar, telemetry systems, radio communication, data transmission and optical tracking. The site also provides over-the-horizon transmitter capability for the flight control of unmanned aircraft systems. Located at a height of more than 1,400ft (427m) overlooking the Pacific Ocean, the site is also home to the US Space Command's 10th Space Operations Squadron (10 SOPS), which assumed control of the former Naval Satellite Operations Center in June 2022. In addition to Laguna Peak, instrumentation and data collection facilities are located at Point Mugu and on San Nicolas and Santa Cruz Islands.

US Secretary of the Navy James V Forrestal first proposed establishing a naval base at Point Mugu in March 1945. In preparation, the Navy began staging key missile testing personnel and equipment at NAS Mojave, California, where a pilotless aircraft unit had been set up. The Point Mugu facility was established as Naval Air Missile Test Center when it stood up on October 1, 1946. It was redesignated as the Naval Missile Test Center (NMC) on January 7, 1959 and the Pacific Missile Test Center (PMTC) on April 26, 1975. Flight operations are conducted from Point Mugu's primary 11,000ft (3,553m) and secondary 5,500ft (1,524m) runways.

Sea Range

NAWCWD Test and Evaluation capabilities include the Point Mugu Sea Range and China Lake Ranges. Located off the coast of California, the Point Mugu Sea Range (PMSR) was originally known as the Pacific Missile Range, when it was established as the Navy's first instrumented missile test sea range on June 16, 1958. Offering geographic diversity, the range includes open ocean, deep water

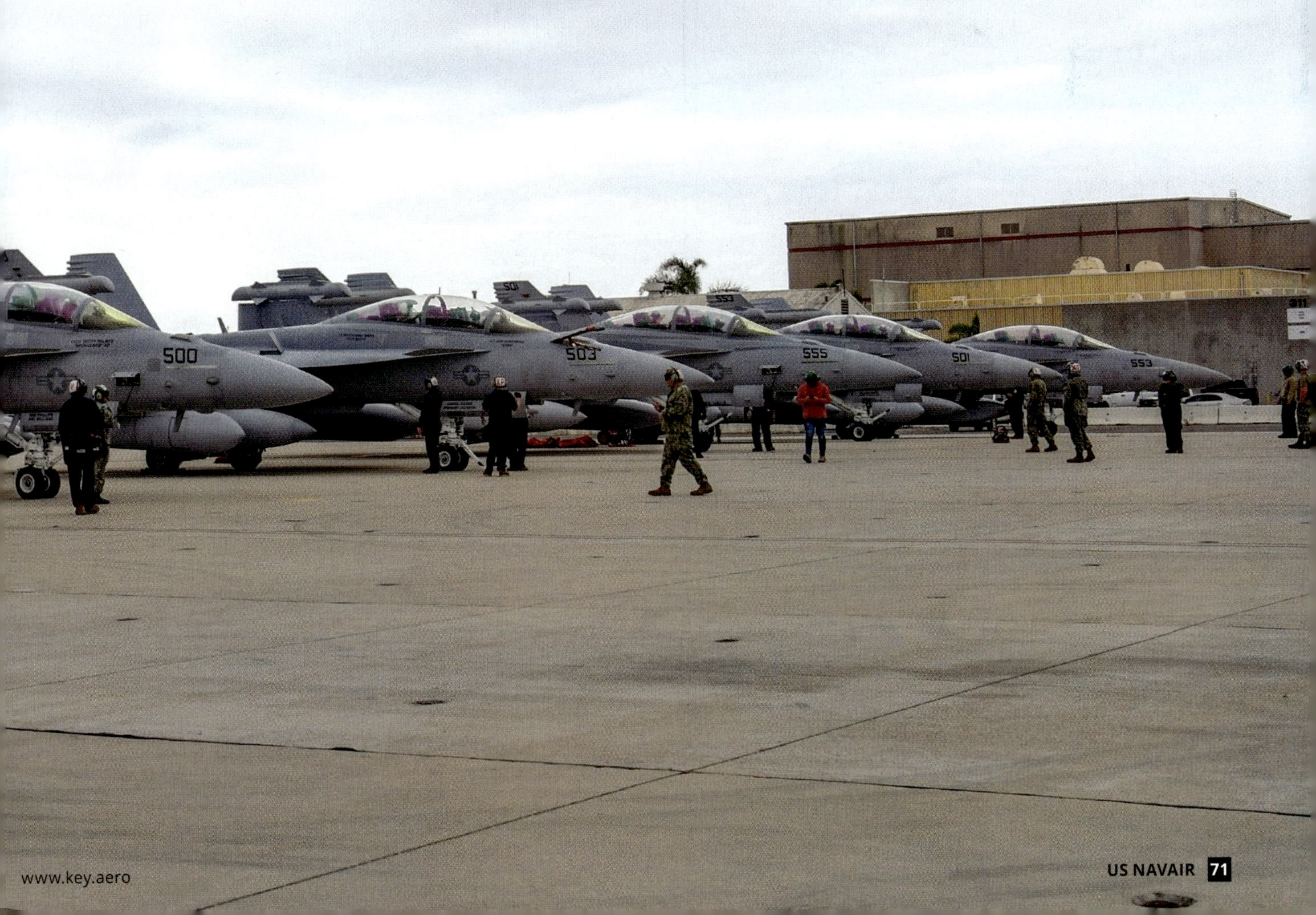

An F/A-18F operated by Air Test and Evaluation Squadron VX-31 fires an AIM-9X Sidewinder air-to-air missile from its wingtip rail during a test over the Point Mugu Sea Range. (US Navy)

ports, and protected islands within restricted air space. It is the nation's largest and most capable instrumented RDT&E sea range. The area provides 125,000 square miles (323,749km²) of instrumented sea range and 36,000 square miles (93,240km²) of controlled overlying airspace, which consists of three 'Restricted' and 11 'Warning Areas' and includes San Nicolas and Santa Cruz Islands. Capable of being expanded to cover 220,000 square miles, (569,797km²), the range supports both developmental and operational test and evaluation of missiles, free-fall weapons and electronic warfare systems. Weapons evaluations include air-to-air, air-to surface, surface-to-surface, surface-to-air and sub-surface-to-surface missiles. In addition to test activities, the range supports fleet training and tactics development, such as large-scale, major exercises including fleet battle experiments. The expansive sea range hosts a variety of high-profile test programmes:

- Aircraft and aerial weapon systems
- Ship and ship self-defence systems
- Cruise missile testing
- Unmanned systems testing
- Combat system ship qualification trials (CSSQT) and fleet training exercises (FLEETEX)
- Hypersonic weapons
- Directed energy systems
- Strategic systems testing

Aerial target systems used on the range include GQM-163 supersonic missiles, BQM-34S and BQM-177A subsonic missiles and a variety of low speed aerial target (LSAT) drones. Operating from the Naval Base's Port Hueneme facility, seaborne powered targets

MQ-8C BuNo 168455 was one of several unmanned Fire Scout helicopters that underwent testing at Naval Base Ventura County Point Mugu, supported by the NAWCWD. (Northrop Grumman)

Wearing a throwback paint scheme honouring the centennial of naval aviation, an F/A-18C from Air Test and Evaluation Squadron VX-31 takes off from Naval Base Ventura County Point Mugu for a training mission on August 10, 2023. The Hornet's paint scheme was inspired by one worn by China Lake test jets during the 1960s. (US Navy/Eric Parsons)

range from the manned or unmanned high speed manoeuvrable surface target (HSMST), fast attack craft target (FACT), mobile ship target (MST), ship deployable surface target (SDST) and the QST-35A/B seaborne target (SEPTAR). Part of the NAWCWD Threat/Target Systems Department (TTSD) at Point Mugu, the Pacific Targets and Marine Operations (PTMO) Division manages the operations of the targets.

San Nicolas Island is located 65 miles (105km) south of Point Mugu and 75 miles (121km) west of Los Angeles in the Pacific Ocean. Facilities include Naval Outlying Field (NOLF) San Nicolas Island, which has a single 11,000ft (3,353m) runway with hangar space and daily scheduled passenger and logistics flights. Owned by the US Navy, the facility is equipped with radar and electro-optical devices tracking telemetry and communication systems. The base also has an impact/ground target area and missile and target build-up, storage and launch facilities that are primarily used for short and medium range missile testing and target launches.

NAVAIR operations on the eastern end of Santa Cruz Island include a leased ten-acre instrumentation complex on a mountain top that supports the Point Mugu Sea Range. The facility collects meteorological data, provides secure VHF/UHF radio communications, relays data and operates surface surveillance radar for the sea range. The solar-powered site includes a heliport, fire station barracks, and other support facilities. The island is owned by the Nature Conservancy and the National Park Service.

China Lake

NAWS China Lake is located near Ridgecrest in the Western Mojave Desert region of California, around 150 miles (241km) northeast of Los Angeles. It is situated in the high desert, near the Sierra Nevada Mountains and the Indian Wells Valley. The installation represents the US Navy's largest single land-holding comprising 85% of the Navy's land for RDT&E operations and 38% of the service's worldwide land-holdings. The station's two ranges and main ▶

A pair of AV-8Bs from Air Test and Evaluation Squadron VX-31 conduct refuelling operations with a USAF KC-46A on September 15, 2022. Based at NAWS China Lake, the 'Dust Devils' flew their final Harrier II mission on September 23, 2025. (US Navy)

A BQM-34 unmanned aerial vehicle launches from NAWS China Lake during a test of the US Navy's SFIRR demonstrator, developed by Naval Air Warfare Center Weapons Division. The test marked the first air launch of SFIRR from an unmanned platform. (US Navy)

site cover more than 1.1 million acres, an area larger than the entire state of Rhode Island.

Jointly controlled by the NAWCWD, the 412th Test Wing at Edwards Air force Base and the US Army's National Training Center (NTC) at Fort Irwin, the R-2508 Airspace Complex includes nearly 20,000 square miles (51,800km²) of special airspace composed of restricted areas, military operations areas (MOAs) and air traffic control assigned airspace (ATCAA).

Located within the China Lake ranges, the electronic combat range supports development and operational testing of airborne electronic warfare systems and tactics against shipboard and land-based air defence systems. The R-2508 Airspace Complex's special airspace comprises restricted areas, military operations areas (MOAs) and air traffic control assigned airspace. The IR-200 low-level route connects the PMSR and the China Lake complex.

Collectively referred to as the China Lake Ranges (CLR), the North and South Ranges are separated by 25 miles (40.2km) of public lands. The North Range supports ground operations that include target development, live-fire bombing tests and unexploded

ordnance and is home to the Range Operations Center where flight and ground tests are conducted. The South Range specialises in electronic warfare, including a full array of integrated threat capabilities.

NAWCWD China Lake traces its history to the establishment of the Naval Ordnance Test Station (NOTS) in November 1943. NOTS was tasked to conduct research, development and testing of weapons, and delivering weapons employment training. Opened in June 1945, the station's airfield was named to honour Navy Lieutenant John Armitage, who was killed during testing at the NOTS in August 1944.

In 1950, scientists and engineers at NOTS developed the air-intercept missile known as the AIM-9 Sidewinder, which has become the world's most used and copied air-to-air missile. Since that time, rockets and missiles developed or tested at China Lake have included the Mighty Mouse, Zuni, Sidewinder, Shrike, Joint Stand-off Weapon (JSOW) and Joint Direct-Attack Munition (JDAM). In July 1967, NOTS China Lake and the Naval Ordnance Laboratory in Corona, California, were combined to form the Naval Weapons Center.

Operations are supported by Air Test & Evaluation Squadron VX-31. Known as the 'Dust Devils', the squadron conducts research, development, test and evaluation (RDT&E) associated with current and future manned aircraft, weapons and weapons systems. Flight operations at Armitage Field are carried out from three runways that measure 11,200ft (3,414m), 10,000ft (3,048m) and 9,014ft (2,747m)

Aerial Targets

The GQM-163 Coyote is a ground-launched supersonic sea-skimming missile (SSSM) target built by Northrop Grumman. Originally developed by Orbital ATK, which was acquired by Northrop Grumman, it succeeded the MQM-8 Vandal. Powered by an Aerojet MARC-R-282 solid-fuel ducted rocket/ramjet engine, the Coyote is launched by a Hercules MK-70 booster. Orbital ATK began developing the GQM-163A under a $34m engineering and manufacturing development (EMD) contract in June 2000. Capable of operating at altitudes from 50-52,000ft (15.2-15,850m) and speeds up to Mach 3.6, the SSSM became operational in October 2005.

A 'Dust Devils' FA-18E taxies back to the ramp at NAWS China Lake following a mission on August 21, 2023. Operated by Air Test and Evaluation Squadron VX-31, the Super Hornet is assigned BuNo 166871. (US Navy)

An F/A-18E assigned to Air Test and Evaluation Squadron VX-31 operates alongside a DC-10-40 tanker operated by Omega Aerial Refueling Services after performing an aerial refuelling test on March 11, 2021. (US Navy)

It is also capable of manoeuvring to simulate current threats facing the fleet and is a critical test and training asset.

The BQM-177A is a ground or ship-launched subscale, high subsonic aerial target that replicates modern subsonic anti-ship cruise missile (ASCM) threats in support of fleet training and developmental/operational testing of major US Department of Defense (DoD) and international weapon systems. It is capable of supporting various mission requirements by carrying a wide array of internal and external payloads. Options include scoring, identification friend-or-foe (IFF), passive active radio frequency (RF) augmentation, infrared (IR) augmentation, electronic countermeasures, chaff and flare dispensing and tow targets. The target can achieve speeds in excess of Mach 0.9 and operate at altitudes as low as 10ft (3.04m), which provides sea-skimming anti-ship cruise missile threat emulation. Produced by Kratos Defense & Security Solutions, the BQM-177A achieved initial operational capability on ▶

NRA-3B BuNo 144825 from the Pacific Missile Test Center awaits its crew for a test mission at NAS Point Mugu on October 11, 1990. The Douglas Skywarrior was the largest aircraft to operate from US Navy aircraft carriers. (Mike Anselmo)

Operated by Air Test and Evaluation Squadron VX-30, one of the US Navy's last P-3C Orions taxies after landing at Naval Base Ventura County Point Mugu on May 11, 2022. Known as the 'Bloodhounds', the squadron is a component of the Naval Air Warfare Center Weapons Division. (US Navy/Ensign Drew Verbis)

One of two E-2D Advanced Hawkeyes operated by Air Test and Evaluation Squadron VX-30, BuNo 168077 returns to Naval Base Ventura County Point Mugu at the conclusion of a mission in May 2023. (US Navy)

A trio of Lockheed Martin S-3Bs from Air Test and Evaluation Squadron VX-30 share the ramp at Naval Base Ventura County Point Mugu with another example operated by the National Aeronautics and Space Administration (NASA) in September 2014. The 'Bloodhounds' were the last US Navy squadron to operate the Viking and retired its last S-3Bs in January 2016. (US Navy/Vance Vasquez)

February 27, 2019. The Pacific Target and Marine Operations Division launched its 200th BQM-177 flight in support of NAWC-WD's China Lake Range on April 2, 2024.

The BQM-34S Firebee is a recoverable, remote-controlled subsonic aerial target. It can operate at speeds up to Mach 0.9 and altitudes from 10ft to 45,000ft (3.04-

One of two P-3C Orions operated by Air Test and Evaluation Squadron VX-30, at Naval Base Ventura County Point Mugu operates alongside the first F-35A Lightning II over the Point Mugu Sea Range during a test mission. *(US Navy)*

13,716m) and perform manoeuvres of up to 5gs. Developed by Teledyne Ryan, it is powered by a single General Electric J85-GE-100A turbojet engine; the target is designed to be ground surface-launched from a short rail or zero length ground-launcher utilising a single jet assisted take-off (JATO) bottle. It is controllable through normal flight and its large payload capacity makes the BQM-34S a highly useful target for fleet training and weapon system research, development test and evaluations. The BQM-34 is produced by Northrop Grumman, which acquired Teledyne Ryan in 1999.

The USAF formally retired the General Atomics MQ-1B Predator in March 2018, but a large number of the remotely piloted aircraft were transferred to NAVAIR. They now serve as aerial targets with NAWCWD, under the designation NMQ-1B. In addition to systems testing, the Predators will serve as target drones to support combat training exercises conducted on the Point Mugu Sea Range. ■

Known as 'Billboard', NP-3D BuNo 150521 was originally delivered to the US Navy in P-3A configuration, but was later modified for a special mission and is currently assigned to Air Test and Evaluation Squadron VX-30 at Naval Base Ventura County Point Mugu. (US Navy)

EA-18G BuNo 169126 conducts a test with the Raytheon Next Generation Jammer Mid-Band (NGJ-MB) pod. The Growler was operated by Air Test and Evaluation Squadron VX-31 and based at NAWS China Lake, California. (US Navy)

THE DESTINATION FOR MILITARY ENTHUSIASTS

KEY Publishing

Visit us today and discover all our publications

SCAN ME

Aviation News is renowned for providing the best coverage of every branch of aviation.

SCAN ME

Airforces Monthly is devoted to modern military aircraft and their air arms.

and subscribe to your favourite magazine...

/collections/subscriptions

Free 2nd class P&P on BFPO orders. Overseas charges apply.

P-3C BuNo 158934 from VX-30 makes its final approach to land at NAS JRB Fort Worth, Texas, during a visit on October 16, 2020. Known as the 'Bloodhounds', the squadron is one of two US Navy units still equipped with Orions. (Keith Snyder)

California Bloodhounds

Air Test and Evaluation Squadron Three Zero (VX-30)

(Air Test and Evaluation Squadron VX-30 Insignia)

Air Test and Evaluation Squadron VX-30 was originally established at Naval Air Station Point Mugu, near Oxnard, California, on May 8, 1995, and was initially designated as Naval Weapons Test Squadron (NTWS) Point Mugu. Known as the 'Bloodhounds', the squadron took on its current identity on May 1, 2002. As a component of the Naval Air Warfare Center Weapons Division, VX-30 reports to NAWCWD's Naval Test Wing Pacific. Prior to its establishment as the NWTS, flight test operations were assigned directly to the Pacific Missile Test Center (PMTC) and its predecessor organisations. Under the PMTC, the aircraft used for project execution were 'detailed' to the Systems Evaluation Directorate/Weapons System Test Department and range support aircraft were assigned to the Range Directorate/Range Operations Department. Logistics and station support aircraft were under the cognisance of the NAS Point Mugu Air Operations Department.

VX-30 is the Naval Air Systems Command's principal naval flight and ground test unit at Naval Base Ventura County – Point Mugu. It supports research, development, test and evaluation (RDT&E) of manned and unmanned fixed and rotary-wing aircraft and weapons systems and the US Navy's Point Mugu Sea Test Range off the shore of central California.

VX-30's customers include the National Reconnaissance Office (NRO), Missile Defense Agency (MDA), Defense Advanced Research Project Agency (DARPA), the US Navy Strategic Systems Program and the Navy's Program Executive Offices (PEO) for Integrated Warfare Systems (PEO-IWS), Unmanned Systems and Weapons (PEO-U&W), Joint Strike Fighter (PEO-JSF) and numerous other US Department of Defense programmes.

During a May 2025 Change of Command ceremony, Captain David Halpern, commodore of Naval Test Wing Pacific, described VX-30 as a "hybrid test and fleet support squadron". It is uniquely equipped with specialised aircraft and range access to deliver operationally ready capabilities. He went on to say: "Without VX-30, many of our most complex test operations wouldn't be possible."

The 'Bloodhounds' aircraft are tasked with an array of missions that include range surveillance, photometric support, area clearance and airborne telemetry on the Naval Air Systems Command's Point Mugu Sea Range. Project officers lead several weapon system developmental test programmes for the fleet. The range surveillance and clearance mission ensures the safety of

QF-4S 158360 is one of a number of Phantom IIs operated as target drones by VX-30 over the Point Mugu Sea Test Range until retired in 2004. (US Navy)

KC-130T BuNo 162311 from VX-30 makes its final approach to land at NAS JRB Fort Worth during a visit on May 21, 2025. The Hercules is one of two operated by the 'Bloodhounds' from Point Mugu. (Keith Snyder)

non-participating vessels or assets permitting live-fire weapons testing to be conducted safely and effectively. Photometric data collected by VX-30 provides high-fidelity multi-spectral imagery for post-flight mission reconstruction and data analysis in support of systems being tested on or over the sea range. The telemetry relay and recording mission has also been key enabler for the execution of high-profile missions conducted from remote locations worldwide.

Operational specialists within the squadron's Range Department are responsible for safety of flight and range clearance over the entire test range of 36,000 square nautical miles. VX-30's Airborne Threat Simulation Detachment routinely deploys worldwide to meet unique weapon testing needs at remote ranges and to provide fleet support. The squadron's Range Operations Department provides tracking and controlling services for surface and airborne targets on the Point Mugu Sea Range.

Responsibility for the squadron is assigned to Commander Barry F Carmody Jr, who assumed command on May 1, 2025.

Test Fleet

At one time tasked with evaluating air-to-air weapons and systems, VX-30's mission was realigned following the conclusion of the US Navy's QF-4 target drone programme and the retirement of its F-14 Tomcats. As a result, the unit's F/A-18s were relocated to Naval Air Weapons Station China Lake and assigned to VX-31. Considered a combat support unit, the squadron's diverse inventory of aircraft includes the Lockheed Martin P-3C and NP-3D Orion and KC-130T Hercules; recent additions added the Northrop Grumman E-2D and Gulfstream NC-20G. ▶

One of two KC-130Ts assigned to VX-20 departs from NAS JRB Fort Worth during a visit on December 7, 2023. The 'Herc', which carries BuNo 162308, was originally delivered to the US Marine Corps and passed along to the 'Bloodhounds' following its replacement by the KC-130J. (Keith Snyder)

F-14D BuNo 163415 from VX-30 flies chase alongside a Tomahawk cruise missile over the Point Mugu sea range during a test mission on November 10, 2002. (US Navy)

Prior to entering service with VX-30 in October 2013, NP-3D BuNo 153442 was originally operated from NAS Patuxent River, Maryland, by the Naval Research Laboratory Flight Support Detachment. The Orion was equipped with the Hawkeye 2000's Lockheed Martin AN/APS-145 airborne early warning (AEW) system, and a co-operative engagement capability (CEC) suite. The Orion was retired in 2017. (US Navy/Vance Vasquez)

The first of two E-2D Advanced Hawkeyes delivered to VX-30, BuNo 168077 taxies at Naval Base Ventura County Point Mugu in March 2024. The aircraft is referred to as 'Bloodhound 600'. (US Navy)

One of two P-3Cs assigned to VX-30, P-3C BuNo 162999 taxies out for a test mission at Naval Base Ventura County Point Mugu. The Orion often uses the callsign 'Bloodhound 300'. (US Navy)

The last of three 'Billboard' NP-3Ds operated by VX-30, 'Bloodhound 341' taxies at Naval Base Ventura County Point Mugu on May 21, 2015. (US Navy)

VX-30 operates a pair of Lockheed Martin KC-130Ts that were originally flown by units of the US Marine Corps Reserve. In addition to logistic support missions, the 'Hercs' provide air refuelling support for test operations being carried out over the sea range. The first of the KC-130Ts assigned to the 'Bloodhounds' received a prototype Starlink connection in September 2024; the squadron's second Hercules was similarly modified in 2025. The system supports beyond-line-of-sight communications and mobile data relay, providing mobile range infrastructure for operations on the Point Mugu Sea Range. The Starlink satellite connectivity enhances the Herc's role supporting missile and weapons testing. Equipped with the satellite communications range extension aircraft modification (SCREAM), one of the KC-130Ts served as a surrogate missile in advance of the US Army's Typhon test during Exercise Talisman Sabre in Australia that took place in July 2025. Operating from the Nackeroo Airfield at the Australian Army's Bradshaw Field Training Area in the Northern Territory, the Hercules simulated the trajectory of an SM-6 standard missile fired from the US Army's mid-range capability portable launcher. The mission enabled ground systems in Australia to test communication, telemetry and tracking before the first actual live missile launch. Installed in 2024, the SCREAM enabled beyond-line-of-sight communications via Starlink and leveraged the aircraft's existing power, RF and GPS systems.

VX-30 and Scientific Developmental Squadron VXS-1 at NAS Patuxent River are responsible for the last Lockheed Martin P-3 Orions operated by the US Navy. The aircraft include two P-3Cs and a single NP-3D, known as 'Bloodhound 341'. The heavily modified Orion, also known as the 'Panel Bird', features a large, dorsal phased-array

Wearing the civil registration N544GD, a heavily modified Gulfstream 550 taxies on August 13, 2018, during a visit to Lambert St Louis International Airport, Missouri. Assigned the designation NC-37B, BuNo 166379 will replace VX-30's NP-3D when it is delivered in 2026. (Mark Munzel)

Originally operated by the US Naval Reserve NC-20G BuNo 165094 was modified as a range support aircraft and is currently assigned to VX-30. (US Navy)

P-3C BuNo 162999 from VX-30 makes its final approach to land on March 23, 2025. 'Bloodhound 300' is one of three Orions assigned to the 'Bloodhounds'. (Mike Wilson)

In May 2023, VX-30 received a modified C-20G Gulfstream IV that had previously served in the Navy Unique Fleet Essential Airlift (NUFEA) mission with Fleet Logistics Support Squadron 51 (VR-51) in Hawaii. Now assigned the designation the NC-20G, it provides range support. The NC-20G is primarily configured to visually document missile tests using the Cast Glance gyro-stabilised imaging system. The system is capable of obtaining precision and/or high-resolution video and still images and transmitting them to a ground-station over extended distances. The Gulfstream is flown by a crew of two naval aviators, one naval flight officer (NFO), one observer and a range support team, and is maintained by civilian contract maintenance personnel.

Although the Navy accepted a Gulfstream 550 on July 30, 2018, the heavily modified aircraft has yet to arrive at Point Mugu. Assigned the designation NC-37B, the new telemetry range support aircraft (TRSA) will replace the last NP-3D that is in service with VX-30. The Gulfstream is equipped with an advanced airborne telemetry instrumentation system developed by the Raytheon Company's missile systems segment in Albuquerque, New Mexico, under a $79.7m contract. Systems include a commercial aircraft-based instrumentation telemetry system (CBITS) and an airborne command transmitter system (ACTS). Assigned the designation NC-37B, the new telemetry range support aircraft (TRSA) will replace VX-30's last NP-3D 'Billboard' range support aircraft. Ordered as a 'green' unfinished airframe from Gulfstream in 2016 at a cost of $91.9m, the NC-37B is now expected to enter service in 2026.

The squadron has operated several unmanned air systems including the General Atomics MQ-1B Predator and Navmar Applied Sciences Corporation (NASC) RQ-23A TigerSharks. After being declared surplus by the USAF, VX-30 acquired a number of Predator remotely piloted aircraft that are used as targets over the sea range and known by the designation NMQ-1B.

VX-30 expects to add another large platform to its inventory when the first Boeing P-8A Poseidon arrives at Point Mugu in 2026. The Poseidon will replace the squadron's remaining P-3Cs and will take on RDT&E duties along with the range support mission. ■

antenna that provides over-the-horizon radar and telemetry tracking during missile testing and range support. The specialised aircraft gathers telemetry data, re-transmits signals and provides surveillance for sea range operations. The NP-3D is equipped with phased array antenna and over-the-horizon telemetry equipment that are used to locate and track targets for weapons testing and missile-range clearance. Built by Lockheed in 1963, the P-3A was third Orion modified to 'Billboard' configuration and equipped with Extended Area Test System (EATS) radar. The other two NP-3Ds were retired in 2006 and 2015. The aircraft will be replaced by a specially configured Gulfstream 550 that is assigned the designation NC-37B.

The squadron received the first of two E-2D Advanced Hawkeyes for mission-system testing in 2022. The acquisition was part of a larger effort to expand the NAWCWD's RDT&E efforts. Equipped with advanced AN/APY-9 active electronically scanned array (AESA) radar and communication systems, the E-2D's arrival supported plans to conduct integrated Carrier Air Wing testing.

An F-14A assigned to the Pacific Missile Test Center conducts a test mission near NAS Point Mugu. Initially assigned to the Naval Missile Center and then PMTC, VX-30 was the last unit at Point Mugu to operate the Tomcat. (US Navy)

China Lake's

Air Test and Evaluation Squadron Three One (VX-31)

Known by the nickname 'Dust Devils', Air Test and Evaluation Squadron VX-31 is stationed near Ridgecrest, California, aboard Naval Air Warfare Station (NAWS) China Lake. Reporting to the Naval Test Wing Pacific, VX-31 is a component of the Naval Air Warfare Center Weapons Division (NAWCWD), which is headquartered at the weapons station.

VX-31 was originally known as Naval Weapons Test Squadron China Lake, when it was established on May 8, 1995. In the earliest days of testing on the base, the aircraft were assigned directly to Naval Air Facility China Lake. However, from 1976 until 1995, aircraft test operations at China Lake were consolidated under the Aircraft Department of the Naval Weapons Center's (NWC) Test & Evaluation Directorate. The 'Dust Devils' took on its current identity on May 1, 2002, when it became known as VX-31. Today, it is the Naval Air Systems Command's principal naval flight test unit at NAWS China Lake.

Personnel assigned to VX-31 comprise test pilots and flight test engineers who perform

AH-1Z BuNo 166759 conducts a mission while assigned to the VX-31 in December 2007. The early production Viper was transferred to VMX-1 at MCAS Yuma, but in January 2021 was placed in storage at Davis-Monthan AFB, Arizona. (US Navy)

Operating from Naval Base Ventura County Point Mugu, EA-18G BuNo 169131 from VX-31 prepares to taxi out from a mission during the annual Gray Flag exercise on September 1, 2024. (US Navy/Katie Archibald)

research, development, test and evaluation (RDT&E) work related to weapons and mission systems. Much of the work carried out by the squadron involves testing software updates to both aircraft and weapons and integration testing of new weapons and weapon load configurations. Known as Software Configuration Sets (SCS), the software updates often provide major capability upgrades. As an example, H18 SCS included several releases providing the F/A-18E/F and EA-18G with enhancements to the AN/APG-79 radar electronic protection, network-centric warfare (NIFC) and infrared search and track (IRST) systems. Additionally, it integrated new weapon systems, including the AGM-158C long-range anti-ship missile (LRASM) and GBU-53/B StormBreaker SDB II (small diameter bomb II). It also enabled the Growler to deploy the NGJ-MB (next-generation jammer – medium band). Its efforts include testing new and upgraded mission systems such as radars, electronic warfare (EW) systems and electro-optical/infrared (EO/IR) sensors. The squadron has been involved in testing new technologies including the joint direct attack munition (JDAM) and other advanced precision weapons.

Wearing a special paint scheme honouring the 100th anniversary of US naval aviation, F/A-18C BuNo 165210 operates over the snow-covered Sierra Nevada mountain range in California alongside F/A-18F BuNo 165668. (US Navy)

Dust Devils

NAWS China Lake was known as the Naval Ordnance Test Station (NOTS) when it was established on November 1, 1943. From July 1, 1967, until January 22, 1992, the facility was called Naval Weapons Center China Lake. The primary function assigned to the NOTS was the research, development and testing of weapons. Scientists and engineers at NOTS were responsible for developing the world's first air-intercept missile. Known as the Sidewinder, the AIM-9 is arguably the world's most successful air-to-air missile. Since then, the China Lake facility has developed or tested numerous other rockets and missiles including the 2.75in (70mm) Mighty Mouse and 5in (127mm) Zuni folding fin aerial rockets (FFAR), AGM-45 Shrike, AGM-154 JSOW and free-fall weapons such as the GPS-guided JDAM.

(Air Test and Evaluation Squadron VX-31 Insignia)

aerial threats, including ballistic missiles in the terminal phase of flight and highly manoeuvrable hypersonic weapons under certain conditions. When used in a quasi-ballistic mode, it can also be used against sea and land-based targets. The AIM-174B provides the Super Hornet with the capability to engage targets at much greater distances than the AIM-120 AMRAAM (advanced medium-range air-to-air missile).

Additionally, the squadron supported live-fire testing of the long-range AIM-260 JATM (joint advanced tactical missile) that will address advanced threats. Under development by Lockheed Martin is the beyond-visual-range air-to-air missile (BVRAAM) that is expected to replace or supplement the AIM-120 as the next air-to-air air-dominance weapon for US services. Development of the AIM-260A began in 2017.

In addition to testing and qualifying new weapons, VX-31 is continuously upgrading and testing fielded air-to-air and air-to-ground weapons including AIM-120 and AIM-9 missiles, the AGM-88 HARM (high-speed anti-radiation missile), AGM-88E AARM (advanced anti-radiation guided missile), AGM-154 joint stand-off weapon (JSOW), AGM-158 joint air-to-surface stand-off missile (JASSM), AGM-84 Harpoon, laser-guided bombs and GPS-guided JDAM (joint direct attack munition).

Whereas VX-23 at NAS Patuxent River normally conducts the initial separation and jettison testing for new and upgraded weapons, VX-31 is tasked with weapons assessment testing. These tests confirm that the weapons accurately hit their intended targets, communicate with the launch platform and are compatible with the aircraft systems.

Once developmental testing is completed, the responsibility for operational testing of the ▶

'Dust Devils' F/A-18F BuNo 166635 flies in formation over Point Mugu's sea range with F/A-18D BuNo 165680 during an exercise on January 5, 2025. (US Navy/Katie Archibald)

AV-8B+ BuNo 164549 from VX-31 conducts a mission over one of NAWS China Lake's bombing ranges in southern California on February 27, 2025. The Harrier II was delivered to the Tillamook Air Museum in Oregon in August 2025. (US Navy/Katie Archibald)

A VX-31 'Dust Devils' EA-18G flies over California's Sierra Nevada mountains during a training mission on January 6, 2025. Assigned BuNo 169131, the Growler was the 12th example produced by Boeing. (US Navy/Katie Archibald)

China Lake is synonymous with weapons testing, which is conducted over the weapons station's ranges, as well as the Point Mugu Sea Range near Naval Base Ventura County Point Mugu. The latter facility was previously home to the air-to-air weapons development that was carried out by VX-30. Testing was rationalised under VX-31 shortly after the US Navy retired the F-14 Tomcats assigned to VX-30.

In 2024, the 'Dust Devils' made important contributions to the initial fielding of AIM-174B 'Gunslinger' air-launched version of the SM-6 (standard missile). The programme was initiated in response to an "emergent Pacific Fleet requirement". Based on the combat-proven ship-launched SM-6 missile, AIM-174 is an air-launched version of the RIM-174 ERAM (standard extended-range active missile). The highly capable multi-purpose missile can engage a variety of

An F/A-18F launches an AIM-9X during a weapons test over the Point Mugu Sea Range. Normally based at NAWS China Lake, BuNo 168370 was operated by the VX-31 'Dust Devils'. *(US Navy/Katie Archibald)*

An EA-18G assigned to the VX-31 'Dust Devils' departs from Naval Base Ventura County Point Mugu on August 30, 2022. Based at Naval Air Weapons Station China Lake, California, VX-31 operates F/A-18E/F Super Hornets and EA-18G Growlers including BuNo 169217. *(US Navy/Lt Jg Drew Verbis)*

new weapon or capability is passed over to the 'Vampires' of VX-9, which is also stationed at NAWS China Lake.

Efforts include evaluating newly upgraded systems and, in 2022, VX-31 conducted the first flight test of a US Marine Corps F/A-18D equipped with the latest AN/APG-79(V)4 AESA (active electronically scanned array) radar.

Responsibility for DT&E associated with the US Marine Corps' Bell AH-1Z Viper and UH-1Y Venom helicopters was realigned under Marine Air Test & Evaluation Squadron HMX-1 at MCAS Yuma, Arizona, in April 2015. VX-31 had operated the Venom and Viper since receiving the first examples in mid-2007.

Routinely flying around 4,000 flight hours each year, the squadron is made up of more than 350 personnel, including over 40 active-duty naval aviators and naval flight officers (NFOs). The fixed-wing aviators are all test pilot school graduates. Military personnel include both sailors and marines and the latter are assigned to the Marine Aviation Detachment China Lake (MADCL).

In addition to its primary testing missions, the VX-31 search and rescue (SAR) team conducts inland SAR operations throughout the high desert and mountains. Providing on-call, round-the-clock SAR support, the team is trained for conducting high-altitude rescues in the rugged terrain of southern California's R-2508 Special Use Airspace Complex ranges and the NAWS China Lake main site that cover more than 1.1 million acres. VX-31's highly skilled medical technicians and rescuers also conduct complex high-angle rescues for civilians in the surrounding high desert and mountain regions.

Marine Corps Lt Col Timothy Burchett assumed command of VX-31 on March 6, 2025. A June 2017 graduate of the US Naval Test Pilot School, he had previously served as the squadron's chief test pilot.

A US Navy EA-18G Growler from VX-31 prepares to refuel from an HC-130J operated by the USAF's 418th Test and Evaluation Squadron at Davis-Monthan AFB, Arizona, during Gray Flag 24, off the Californian coast; EA-18G BuNo 169217 was supporting the annual exercise on September 18, 2024. *(USAF/A1C Jasmyne Bridgers-Matos)*

A pair of AV-8B+s from VX-31 deliver inert Mk82 AIR (air inflatable retarder) bombs during a mission over NAWS China Lake on February 27, 2025. The Harrier IIs comprise BuNo 164129 (nearest), which made VX-31's final AV-8B flight on September 23, 2025 and BuNo 164549. The latter aircraft was delivered to the Tillamook Air Museum in Oregon in August 2025. *(US Navy/Katie Archibald)*

A formation of VX-31 'Dust Devils' aircraft, including an AV-8B+, two F/A-18Es and an EA-18G operate over the Point Mugu Sea Range during an exercise on January 9, 2025. (US Navy/Katie Archibald)

Test Fleet

Much like VX-23 at NAS 'Pax' River, VX-31 and its predecessor organisations operated a varied fleet of aircraft. As the US Navy reduced the number of different platforms on its inventory, the variety of aircraft was reduced and just three basic aircraft models are now assigned to the 'Dust Devils'. Operating from China Lake's Armitage Field, VX-31's test aircraft include the Boeing F/A-18E/F Super Hornet, the EA-18G Growler and until recently the Boeing AV-8B Harrier II. In fact, the squadron's last Harrier II flight was carried out on September 23, 2025. VX-31 conducted its final developmental test mission with the AV-8B on June 2, 2025, at China Lake, California. The flight brought an end to 40 years of testing of the Harrier at NAWS China Lake. In the weeks leading up to the final Harrier flight, several of the squadron's jets were delivered to aviation museums, including the Castle Air Museum in California and the Tillamook Air Museum in Oregon.

Super Hornet testing at NAWS China Lake has been carried out for more than 25 years. The first Boeing Super Hornet was delivered to VX-31's predecessor organisation in February 2000, when a two-seat F/A-18F was delivered to the Naval Weapons Test Squadron. EA-18G testing at China Lake began following the arrival of the squadron's first Growler in December 2017. VX-31's Growlers have recently been supporting development of the AN/ALQ-249 NGJ-MB, which is currently being fielded to the EA-18G fleet. The pod, which was developed by Raytheon, achieved initial operational capability in December 2024.

Three Sikorsky MH-60S Seahawks are flown by VX-31's SAR team. Prior to receiving the early production Seahawks in September 2011 the SAR flight was equipped with SH-60Fs. The de-configured anti-submarine warfare Seahawks had replaced China Lake's HH-1N beginning in December 2007. ■

An NEA-18G from VX-31 fires an AGM-88 high-speed anti-radiation missile over the Point Mugu Sea Range in southern California, on July 1, 2008. Originally built as the 135th F/A-18F, BuNo 166642 was later modified to become the second EA-18G. (US Navy)

VX-31 FA-18F BuNo 166968 conducts a test mission over the Point Mugu Sea Range carrying an inert AGM-84 Harpoon anti-ship missile November 18, 2015. (US Navy)

In addition to its DT&E missions, VX-31 is responsible for conducting search and rescue support at NAWS China Lake. The Dust Devils operates three early production MH-60S Seahawks including BuNo 165763. (US Navy)

Fleet Testers

US Navy and Marine Corps Operational Test Squadrons

Working hand-in-hand with the US Navy's developmental air test and evaluation squadrons are three that are tasked with conducting operational test and evaluation (OT&E). Rather than being assigned to the Naval Air Systems Command, the units are aligned under the US Navy Director, Operational Test and Evaluation Force (OPTEVFOR).

As the Navy's independent operational test agency, OPTEVFOR evaluates the effectiveness, suitability and cyber survivability of US Navy, Marine Corps and Coast Guard system capabilities. OPTEVFOR also supports Joint, Multi-Service and Missile Defense Agency cross-service programme capability development. Headquartered at Naval Support Activity (NSA) Hampton Roads in Norfolk, Virginia, the OPTEVFOR provides objective evaluations of aviation systems in support of acquisition and fleet introduction decisions.

The command's Aviation Warfare Division is responsible for planning and executing operational evaluation of aviation acquisition

(VMX-1 Insignia)

Normally based at NAS Patuxent River in Maryland, E-2D BuNo 168600 from Air Test and Evaluation Squadron VX-1, departs from Naval Base Ventura County Point Mugu, California, on September 11, 2025. The Hawkeye was participating in Gray Flag 2025, which is the naval aviation test community's premier large-force test event. (US Navy/MC2 John T Jarrett)

An E-2D assigned to Air Test and Evaluation Squadron VX-1 taxies to its recovery position at Naval Base Ventura County Point Mugu on July 26, 2019. VX-1 is tasked to test and evaluate airborne anti-submarine warfare weapon systems, airborne strategic weapon systems and support systems, equipment and materials in an operational environment. (US Navy/MC2 Victoria Kinney)

(VX-1 Insignia)

A US Navy EA-18G assigned to the Air Test and Evaluation Squadron VX-9 and a US Marine Corps F-35B of Marine Operational Test and Evaluation Squadron VMX-1, prepare to receive fuel from a Royal Air Force KC-30 Voyager during Exercise Northern Edge 23-1 at Joint Base Elmendorf-Richardson, Alaska, on May 9, 2023. (USAF/A1C Shelimar Rivera Rosado)

programmes to assess their operational effectiveness and suitability. Testing is carried out for maritime aircraft and helicopters, unmanned air systems and strike/fighter aircraft, and includes associated weapon systems, electronic warfare (EW) systems, air antisubmarine warfare (ASW) systems, aviation maintenance and training systems. Originally known as the Operational Development Force, US Atlantic Fleet when it was created in December 1947, the agency assumed its current title in May 1959.

Testing is conducted by field activities including Air Test and Evaluation Squadrons VX-1 at Naval Air Station Patuxent River, Maryland, VX-9 at Naval Air Weapons Stations (NAWS) China Lake and VX-9 Detachment Point Mugu at Naval Base Ventura County-Point Mugu, California, and Marine Operational Test and Evaluation Squadron VMX-1 at Marine Corps Air Station (MCAS) Yuma, Arizona.

The squadrons independently assess the effectiveness and suitability of new naval weapons systems and tactics before they are fielded to the operational fleet. Testing is conducted in realistic environments designed to verify the systems function as intended. Their role places the squadrons in a unique position as the interface unit between the development of new weapon and mission systems and subsequent introduction to the fleet.

The results provide the Chief of Naval Operations (CNO) and the acquisition community with data that supports decision-making and improves the combat readiness of Navy warfighters.

'Pioneers'

Stationed at NAS Patuxent River, Maryland, Air Test and Evaluation Squadron VX-1 is tasked with testing and evaluating airborne anti-submarine warfare (ASW) and maritime anti-surface warfare (SUW) weapon systems, airborne strategic weapon systems and support systems, equipment and materials in an operational environment. Additionally, the squadron develops, reviews and disseminates new ASW/SUW tactics and procedures for fleet use. ▶

A flight comprising a US Navy F/A-18F and F-35C from Air Test and Evaluation Squadron VX-9 and an F-15E from the USAF's 422nd Test and Evaluation Squadron fly over the Point Mugu Sea Range in Southern California during the Gray Flag 2024 exercise on September 24, 2024. (US Navy/Lt Cmdr Kory Hughs)

US Marines assigned to Marine Operational Test and Evaluation Squadron VMX-1 conduct maintenance on an F-35B Lighting II during exercise Gray Flag 2024 at Naval Base Ventura County Point Mugu on September 20, 2024. (USMC/LCpl Christian Radosti)

F/A-18F BuNo 166673 operated by Air Test and Evaluation Squadron VX- 9, departs from Naval Base Ventura County Point Mugu, California, on September 11, 2025. The Super Hornet was participating in the naval aviation test community's Exercise Gray Flag 2025. (US Navy/MC2 John T Jarrett)

A member of the Marine Security Force practises fast rope exercises from an MH-60S assigned to the 'Pioneers' Squadron VX-1 at NAS Patuxent River on March 16, 2004. (US Navy/Jim Jenkins)

Operational aircraft assigned to VX-1 include the Boeing P-8A Poseidon, Northrop Grumman E-2D Advanced Hawkeye, Sikorsky MH-60R and MH-60S Seahawk. Additionally, VX-1 provides test and evaluation support for other programmes that include the Boeing E-6B Mercury, Lockheed Martin KC-130J Hercules and Northrop Grumman MQ-4C Triton UAS.

Known as the 'Pioneers', VX-1 was established at NAS Quonset Point, Rhode Island, as part of Air Antisubmarine Commander Air Force, Atlantic Fleet on September 17, 1943, and was known initially as the Air Division of Antisubmarine Development Detachment Atlantic Fleet (ASDEVLANT).

The unit was renamed Antisubmarine Development Squadron One in 1946 and relocated to NAS Key West's Boca Chica Field, Florida. It has been operationally assigned to the OPTEVFOR since 1959. In its role, the squadron was tasked to test and evaluate ASW and related equipment, determine the practical value of such material, and develop and co-ordinate ASW tactics using optimally developed equipment.

On September 15, 1973, VX-1 relocated from NAS Key West to its current home at NAS Patuxent River in Maryland. Although its role has been revised over the years, the principal mission of VX-1 today is testing airborne ▶

An MV-22B from Marine Operational Test and Evaluation Squadron VMX-1 demonstrates its vertical take-off and landing capabilities as part of the Yuma Airshow in Arizona on March 15, 2025. (USMC/LCpl Janell B Alvarez)

MH-60R BuNo from Air Test and Evaluation Squadron VX-1 makes its approach to land at NAS Patuxent River, Maryland, on November 7, 2020. The 'Pioneers' operate both the MH-60R and MH-60S versions of the Seahawk. (US Navy)

Marines from 3rd Battalion, 2nd Marine Regiment, 2nd Marine Division conduct fast rope training with UH-1Y BuNo 169247 during a weapons and tactics instructor course at the US Army Yuma Proving Ground on October 4, 2023. *(USMC/LCpl Eric Dmochowski)*

(VX-9 Insignia)

ASW, maritime anti-surface warfare (ASUW) and airborne command and control platforms (C2) and support systems.

VX-1 continues to evaluate new technology and tactical development of airborne systems that also include extended-range surface/land attack, ASW mining techniques, airborne mine countermeasures (AMCM) and EW along with hunter/killer anti-submarine tactics.

Captain Clif 'Cornbread' Coleman assumed command of the 'Pioneers' on June 27, 2025.

Although it reports operationally to the Aviation Warfare Division of OPTEVFOR, VX-1 is administratively assigned to the Commander Patrol Reconnaissance Group Atlantic (COMPATRECONGRULANT) at NSA Hampton Roads.

'Vampires'

Known as the 'Vampires', VX-9 was formally established at Naval Air Weapons Station (NAWS) China Lake, California, through a merger of the former VX-4 and VX-5, on April 1, 1994. Stationed at NAS Point Mugu and China Lake, respectively, the two squadrons had both been tasked with operational testing as part of the OPTEVFOR.

Established as Air Development Squadron VX-5 at NAS Moffett Field, California, the 'Vampires' relocated to Naval Air Facility China Lake in July 1956, where it primarily supported evaluations of air-to-ground weapons and delivery platforms. Nicknamed 'Evaluators', Air Development Squadron VX-4 was established at Point Mugu on September 11, 1952, and was primarily tasked with air-to-air weapons evaluations. VX-4 and VX-5 were redesignated as Air Test and Evaluation Squadrons in January 1969 when they were aligned under the OPTEVFOR.

Although headquartered at China Lake, following its establishment, VX-9 stood up a detachment at Point Mugu. Flight operations from Point Mugu were consolidated at China Lake following the retirement of 'Vampires' F-14s in 2004.

Today, VX-9 is charged with operational evaluation of attack, fighter and electronic warfare aircraft, weapons systems and equipment in direct support of naval aviation fleet squadrons. Additionally, the squadron develops tactical procedures for employing those assets. The squadron operates Boeing F/A-18E, F/A-18F Super Hornets and EA-18G Growlers.

In October 2011, the unit established a detachment at Edwards Air Force Base, California, where it carries out operational

Director, Operational Test & Evaluation Force (OPTEVFOR) – NSA Hampton Roads, Virginia Aviation Warfare Division – NSA Hampton Roads			
Unit	**Location**	**Aircraft**	**Tail Code**
VX-1 'Pioneers' (Note 1)	NAS Patuxent River, Maryland	MH-60R/S, E-2D, P-8A	JA
VX-9 'Vampires' (Note 2)	NAWS China Lake, California	EA-18G, F/A-18C/D/E/F	XE
VMX-1 'Flying Lions' (Note 3)	MCAS Yuma, Arizona	AH-1Z, UH-1Y, CH-53K, MV-22B, F-35B, MQ-9A	MV

Notes
1 VX-1 is under the ADCON of COMPATRECONGRULANT
2 VX-9 is under the ADCON of COMSTRIKFIGHTWINGPAC
3 VMX-1 is under the ADCON of the deputy commandant for aviation (DCA)

testing of the F-35C version of the Lightning II alongside USAF units that are responsible for F-35A OT&E.

VX-9 Detachment Edwards began flying the F-35C in 2017 and supported the initial operational test and evaluation of the Lightning II as part of the Joint Strike Fighter Operational Test Team.

VX-9 also reports operationally to the Aviation Warfare Division of OPTEVFOR. However, it is administratively assigned to the Commander, Stike Fighter Wing Pacific (COMSTRKFIGHTWINGPAC) at NAS Lemoore, California. Captain Charles D Fairbank assumed command of VX-9 on March 21, 2024.

'Flying Lions'

MCAS Yuma, Arizona, is home to Marine Operational Test and Evaluation Squadron VMX-1, which conducts operational tests of all US Marine Corps aviation systems, including fixed-wing, tiltrotor and rotary-wing aircraft, as well as unmanned aerial systems (UAS), to assess their effectiveness, suitability and survivability in realistic combat conditions prior to their deployment. Additionally, it is tasked with tactics development.

The unit was originally known as Marine Tiltrotor Operational Test and Evaluation Squadron VMX-22, when it was activated at MCAS New River, North Carolina, on August 28, 2003. VMX-22 relocated to MCAS Yuma in June 2015 and gradually assumed the OT&E role for the Marine Corps. As a result, several aircraft that had been assigned to VX-9 were relocated from NAWS China Lake to MCAS Yuma, joining the squadron's

Assigned to VX-9's detachment at Edwards AFB, F-35C BuNo 170540 departs from Naval Base Ventura County, Point Mugu, California, on September 12, 2025, during the premier large-force test exercise, Gray Flag 2025, which is conducted annually for the naval aviation test community. (US Navy/Katie Archibald)

MV-22B Ospreys. Those types included the Boeing AV-8B Harrier II, Bell UH-1Y Venom and AH-1Z Viper. A detachment at Edwards AFB received its first F-35B on October 9, 2014.

Known as the 'Flying Lions', VMX-1 took on its current designation on May 13, 2016. In October 2019, the squadron's F-35B detachment relocated from Edwards to Yuma. Although VMX-1 doesn't currently operate the F-35C, the squadron collaborates with VX-9 to ensure USMC requirements are covered. Operational testing of the Sikorsky CH-53K helicopter relocated from MCAS New River, North Carolina, to Yuma when the first King Stallion arrived on June 7, 2024. Like its US Navy counterparts, VMX-1 is operationally aligned under the OPTEVFOR, but administratively it reports to the deputy commandant for aviation. Colonel John 'Ike' Dirk has commanded VMX-1 since October 21, 2024. ■

The first live-fire test of an AIM-120 missile released from an operational F-35 Lightning II was carried out by the Joint Operational Test Team on January 24, 2019. The missile was deployed from the internal weapons storage bay of F-35C BuNo 168842 over the Point Mugu Sea Range off the coast of southern California. (USAF/Christopher Okula)

Airborne Scientists

Scientific Development Squadron One (VXS-1)

Reporting to the US Naval Research Laboratory (NRL) in Washington DC, Scientific Development Squadron VXS-1 conducts airborne scientific experimentation and advanced technology development from its base at Naval Air Station (NAS) Patuxent River, Maryland. Operations take place worldwide in support of US Navy and national science and technology (S&T) priorities and war-fighting goals.

VXS-1 bridges the gap between the laboratory and the fleet, accelerating naval airborne innovation by transforming lab breakthroughs into maritime dominance. The squadron tests advanced technologies ranging from advanced sensors to electronic warfare to ensure US Naval forces maintain a decisive advantage over their enemies.

Known as the 'Warlocks', the squadron traces its history to the activation of the NRL's Flight Support Detachment in January 1963. Formally designated as VXS-1 on December 13, 2004, the 'Warlocks' carry airborne S&T missions in direct support of the Office of Naval Research (ONR) and NRL airborne research projects.

Although it supports broadly based, multi-disciplinary programmes across the full spectrum of scientific research and applied technologies, the squadron is focused on the maritime application of new and improved airborne data collection techniques, experimental equipment and system demonstration.

Recent projects include support for NRL Tactical Electronic Warfare, Optical Sciences, Space Systems, Radar and Ocean Sciences Divisions, Naval Air System's Command (NAVAIR) Advanced Concepts Division, Massachusetts Institute of Technology's (MIT) Lincoln Laboratory and the US Naval Test Pilot School. The squadron has completed S&T research detachments around the globe, including operations in the US Central Command, US European Command and US Indo-Pacific Command areas of responsibility and locally from locations in the continental US.

(VXS-1 Insignia)

US Naval Research Laboratory's Scientific Development Squadron VXS-1 is tasked with conducting airborne scientific experimentation and advanced technology development; the squadron operates four aircraft including the RC-12M, NP-3C and UV-18A. (US Navy/Sarah Peterson)

One of two NP-3C Orions operated by VXS-1, BuNo 158912 taxies at NAS Patuxent River, Mayland, on October 15, 2014. The letter N in the aircraft's designation indicates it has been permanently modified for test duties. The Orion can be rapidly configured to integrate science and technology projects. (US Navy)

Between 2006 and 2017, the US Navy conducted evaluations of an A-170 series Blimp manufactured by the American Blimp Corporation. Assigned the designation MZ-3A, the manned airship was assigned to VXS-1 and operated as an advanced flying laboratory used to evaluate affordable sensor payloads and provide support for other related science and technology projects for the naval research enterprise. (US Navy/John F Williams)

First delivered to the Alaska Army National Guard, UV-18A 79-23255 is assigned to the VXS-1 and normally based at NAS 'Pax River'. The Twin Otter made a steep approach to land at Easton Airport-Newnam Field in Easton, Maryland, during a visit on March 16, 2022. (Sunil Gupta)

The unit has also conducted tasks in support of the US Forest Service, US Geological Survey, National Science Foundation and the National Oceanic and Atmospheric Administration (NOAA).

The squadron has been called on to fly research missions in support of Operations Desert Storm, Enduring Freedom and Iraqi Freedom. Its 2006 NP-3D deployment to Afghanistan as part of Project Rampant Lion, marked the first-ever deployment of a US Navy S&T unit to a combat theatre.

Aircraft

Since is activation as the NRL FSD, VXS-1 has operated a number of different aircraft types, including the Douglas R4D Skytrain, Lockheed EC-121 Constellation and Grumman S-2 as well as several variants of the Lockheed P-3. ▶

RC-12M BuNo 163846 operated by VXS-1 makes its approach to land at St Mary's County Regional Airport, Maryland, on August 3, 2020. The King Air is one of four aircraft operated by the squadron from its base at nearby NAS Patuxent River. (Mike Wilson)

Located at NAS 'Pax River', the US Naval Research Laboratory's Scientific Development Squadron VXS-1 added UV-18A 79-23255 to its small fleet of science and technology research aircraft in May 2019. Originally passed from the US Army Parachute Team, the 'Golden Knights', to the US Naval Postgraduate School, the Twin Otter was subsequently assigned to the 'Warlocks'. (US Navy/NRL)

Departing Easton Airport-Newnam Field on March 16, 2022, UV-18A 79-23255 was originally delivered to the Alaska Army National Guard. Today it is assigned to the VXS-1, based at NAS Patuxent River, Maryland. (Sunil Gupta)

The US Naval Research Laboratory's Scientific Development Squadron VXS-1 added a UV-18A to its inventory of test aircraft in May 2019. Originally operated by the Alaska Army National Guard, the Twin Otter is now based at NAS 'Pax River'. (US Navy/Jonathan Steffen)

In support of its missions, the highly specialised squadron operates and maintains two Lockheed Martin NP-3C Orion aircraft and single examples of the Beechcraft RC-12M Huron, de Havilland Canada UV-18A Twin Otter and a number of Navmar Applied Sciences Corporation (NASC) RQ-23A TigerShark unmanned air systems as airborne scientific research and technology development platforms. Commander Luis A Levine assumed command of VXS-1 at 'Pax River' on November 14, 2024.

Each of VXS-1's aircraft is uniquely modified to support the equipment required for scientific research, such as magnetic variation mapping, hydro-acoustic research, bathymetry, electronic countermeasures, gravity mapping and radar research.

VXS-1's UV-18A Twin Otter was originally operated by the Alaska Army National Guard and later transferred to the US Army Parachute Team 'Golden Knights'. It entered service with the 'Warlocks' in 2019. Modifications made to the short take-off and landing aircraft include port and starboard bubble windows, ports in the nose to accommodate multiple downward-looking sensors or an EO/IR turret. A large aft fuselage cut-out is designed to mount sensor packages such as radar, optical, turrets, etc. Additionally, the aircraft can be configured with a freefall sonobuoy deployment chute and removable wing pylon stations capable of carrying atmospheric or other sensors. The interior can be configured to support equipment racks and workstations.

Originally operated as a range surveillance aircraft (RANSAC) from Naval Station Roosevelt Roads in Puerto Rico, VXS-1's RC-12M has been modified to rapidly integrate smaller science and technology projects. Originally equipped with the Litton Systems Canada, now Northrop Grumman AN/APS-140 sea search radar, the aircraft can be fitted with sensors installed in the empty belly radome and the cabin is rapidly configurable for equipment racks and workstations.

A pair of NP-3Cs provide the capability to carry sensors in the nose and tail radomes and a configurable bomb bay equipment platform can be outfitted with a spherical radome. The aircraft also has the ability to mount sensors externally and to drop sonobuoys from an unpressurised chute.

NP-3C BuNo 158570 from VXS-1 received a series of modifications including the installation of the SnowSAR dual frequency synthetic aperture radar system to support the NASA-led SnowEx 2017 campaign in February 2017. Operations were conducted from Peterson AFB, Colorado. (US Navy/VXS-1)

One of two NP-3Cs operated by VXS-1 awaits its next mission at NAS Patuxent River, Maryland, on October 28, 2016. Originally delivered in the initial P-3C configuration, BuNo 158570 was later modified to Update IIIR capability. (Mike Wilson)

The aircraft provide a heavier lift capability compared with the UV-18A and RC-12M and offer increased range and mission duration. The large cabin can support multiple equipment racks and operator workstations.

Developed by Navmar Applied Sciences Corporation (NASC) in the early 2000s, the RQ-23A TigerShark is a medium-altitude long-endurance UAS. It was first deployed in Iraq and Afghanistan, beginning in 2006, and supported intelligence, surveillance and reconnaissance tasks flying more than 10,000 missions. VXS-1 operates its TigerSharks as scientific and technological testing platforms. ∎

Originally operated as a range support aircraft at Naval Station Roosevelt Roads, Puerto Rico, RC-12F BuNo 163846 now supports scientific experiments and testing carried out by VXS-1 from its base at NAS 'Pax River'. (Mike Wilson)